Understanding Evil

Understanding Evil
Lessons from Bosnia

KEITH DOUBT

FORDHAM UNIVERSITY PRESS
NEW YORK 2006

Copyright © 2006 Fordham University Press

All rights reserved. No part of this publication may be reproduced, stored in a retrieval system, or transmitted in any form or by any means—electronic, mechanical, photocopy, recording, or any other—except for brief quotations in printed reviews, without the prior permission of the publisher.

Library of Congress Cataloging-in-Publication Data

Doubt, Keith.
  Understanding evil : lessons from Bosnia / Keith Doubt.—1st ed.
    p. cm.
  Includes bibliographical references and index.
  ISBN-13: 978-0-8232-2700-6
  ISBN-10: 0-8232-2700-6
  1. Social justice—Bosnia and Hercegovina. 2. War crimes—Bosnia and Hercegovina. 3. Crimes against humanity—Bosnia and Hercegovina. 4. Yugoslav War, 1991–1995—Atrocities—Bosnia and Hercegovina. 5. Good and evil.
  I. Title.
HN639.Z9M636 2006
949.703—dc22
                                                    2006031868

Printed in the United States of America
08 07 06   5 4 3 2 1
First edition

Contents

Acknowledgments   vii

PART 1
Witnessing Evil

"Sea" by Mak Dizdar   1

    1 Evil as Action   3
    2 Evil's Direction   8
    3 Evil's Reason   16
    4 Evil's Vanity   25
    5 Rape as Evil   35
    6 Evil's Agency   39
    7 Evil's Disfigurement of Language   52

PART 2
Understanding Evil

"Paths" by Mak Dizdar   63

    8 Postmodernism's Relation to Evil   65
    9 Psychologizing Evil   80
    10 Ritualizing Evil   91
    11 Theorizing Evil with Socratic Naiveté   107
    12 Sociocide: A New Paradigm for Evil   119

"Lilies" by Mak Dizdar   137

    References   139
    Index   147

Acknowledgments

The kindness of numerous people helped me prepare this book. I am grateful to Maureen Fry, Kenneth Irwin, Adnan Šešić, Abbe Linscott, Brianne Barclay, Luisa Lang Owen, Omer Hadžiselimović, Katherine Westlund, Elizabeth Narcho, Anne Gohmann, and Jessica Gegel. Several generous grants from Wittenberg University allowed me to conduct this research. Enver Dizdar graciously granted Fordham University Press permission to publish the poetry of Mak Dizdar.

Part 1
Witnessing Evil

Sea

On the palm of a hand
a flower

On the palm of a hand
a shower

On the palm of a hand
a hailstone

And
you

You only
worry

about your
worry

Without
worry

—Mak Dizdar
Translated by Luisa Lang Owen and Keith Doubt

1. Evil as Action

> That word *iniquity* strikes awe in its title, but under all the storm and lightning, there is nothing.
>
> —Jorge Luis Borges

Evil is easy to understand empirically. The vast literature on, for example, the Holocaust makes evil accessible and exoteric; memoirs, documentaries, literature, art, and cinema clearly bear witness to what evil is. Evil, however, is difficult to comprehend conceptually. Theoretically evil is abstruse and esoteric.

Plato's Socrates avoids discussing evil, and it is important to understand why. No one knowingly does wrong, Socrates asserts. When someone knows that an act is wrong (truly knows that it is wrong), he or she does not willingly commit the act. Doing wrong, according to Socrates, is a matter of ignorance—a matter of not knowing what is right and nothing more (Plato 1960).

Aristotle understands the reason behind Socrates' refusal to theorize evil; to start *Nicomachean Ethics*, Aristotle writes, "Every art and every inquiry, and similarly every action and pursuit, is thought to aim at some good; and for this reason the good has been rightly declared to be that at which all things aim" (quoted in Blum 1978, 1). In order for action to be action, action aims at some good. This then is the Socratic problem with evil: If evil is action, toward what end does evil aim?

An earlier version of this chapter appeared in *Sociologija nakon Bosne*.

Insofar as evil is action, it, too, must aim at some good. If evil, however, is truly evil, it cannot aim at some good. In order for evil to be what it is, it must aim at what is not good. Once evil becomes action—that is, once evil aims at some good, however poorly conceived or demented—it is no longer evil. It is action that is ignorant of what is good.

What is action and who studies action? As the divine is the subject of theology, justice the subject of jurisprudence, and numbers the subject of mathematics, action is the subject of sociology. Sociology explains what people are doing and why they are doing it. With *The Structure of Social Action*, Talcott Parsons (1968) demonstrates this lesson to the discipline of modern sociology in a compelling way, but the profundity of the lesson is seldom recognized. As a unit of analysis, action is composed of five distinct but interdependent parts. These parts are (1) an actor, (2) a scene, (3) a purpose, (4) a means, and, finally, (5) the act itself motivated by a normative orientation. The first element corresponds to the question "who," the second to the question "where," the third to the question "why," the fourth to the question "how," and the last to the question "what" (Burke 1969). By separating the different elements of action from their natural unity and reconstructing the different elements to see how they are interdependent as a whole, sociologists account for action where action, in contrast to behavior, is the substance of the social.

Different social sciences focus on different elements of the act. Historians, for example, explain the scene of the act, the historical context in which actions occur. Since Bosnia has a complex and intriguing history, historical accounts of Bosnia are challenging as well as competitive. Historical accounts dramatize the question of where the action occurred; historical accounts more or less dominate the explanation of what people were doing and why they were doing it in Bosnia during the recent war. Psychologists explain who the actor is; they address the agent of the act. They explain the nature of the actor's personality and its socialization. Psychologists might analyze the personalities of Radovan Karadžić or Slobodan Milošević and how their dysfunctional upbringings contributed to their pathological conduct.

Political scientists explain the instrument of the act and measure the degree to which the instrument is effective or rational. Political scientists explain how the act occurred and critique the means that were employed. Were war crimes that unconscionably brutalized a group of people and the communities in which they lived in an effective means for achieving a political end? Political scientists objectively and rationally address questions regarding power and authority.

Philosophy explains the purpose of action. It addresses why the action is meaningful, explaining the relationship between the purpose of the act and the agent or the relationship between the purpose of the act and its conditions. Is nationalism a sufficient ideology to support nation-state formation and sustain viable communities? As critical theory, philosophy analyzes the ideology of action.

When it is at its best, sociology comparatively considers the different elements of action and analyzes the dynamics between them. Note the difference between psychology and sociology. Psychology studies behavior, whether it is animal or human, whereas sociology studies action. What is the difference between behavior and action? Psychology and sociology employ different interpretative paradigms to understand the identical subject. Psychologists study why a specific condition leads to a specific behavior or why this upbringing creates that personality. Sociologists as well address these questions, but sociologists also attempt to address the normative orientation of action that guides "the choice of alternative means to an end, in so far as the situation allows alternatives" (Parsons 1968, 44). When the situation allows alternative means or alternative ends, the actor chooses even if the choice is to not choose. We cannot adequately understand action unless we consider all its elements and the role of choice in the collection and particular gathering of these elements. Within the structure of every action, there is a degree of autonomy and creativeness.

Choice is an essential feature of what action is. It is possible to understand behavior without knowing the choices that the subject makes; it, however, is not possible to understand action without knowing the choices that the subject makes. Understanding the motives behind an action is the way we explain the choices of actors as oriented to some normative order. To understand behavior, it is not necessary to know the motive that guided the behavior. Behavior then is a subset of action where the role of choice is not addressed. The action of a criminal, for instance, may be compared with and reduced to the behavior of an animal where the choice of the criminal becomes an irrelevant variable for understanding the criminal's behavior.

With respect to understanding crimes against humanity in Bosnia, it is a mistake to characterize these crimes as aggression. However descriptively accurate this characterization may be, aggression is what animals and humans do when they think that the situation allows no alternatives. Animals are incapable of self-reflection; they do not make decisions based on reasoning and normative orientations. When we say that humans act aggressively, we conceal from ourselves and from others the choices that the actors make. We reduce action to behavior, and we only partially understand what people are doing and why they are doing it.

To understand what happened to people in Bosnia during the war between 1992 and 1995 is formidable. If we remain dissatisfied with historical, journalistic, psychological, political, philosophical, and sociological accounts of what people were doing and why during the war in Bosnia, it may be because the accounts remain reductionistic. They address the behavior rather than the action of the subject. They sensationalize the former and mask the latter. The subject remains invisible as a member of society, although the question of his or her membership is a matter of great interest. It is, after all, action rather than behavior from which we develop significant knowledge of society. Normative orientations, inherited from society and mediated by culture, inform the choices of actors; normative orientations provide the character of motivated action. Through the study of action, we learn about the substance of society.

It is, after all, action rather than behavior from which we gain moral understanding. No matter how scientifically understood, behavior provides no moral lessons and teaches us little about ourselves. It is action that gives moral lessons with respect to the principled understanding of social life. The world cherishes literature and cinema for the stories they tell because such stories narrate actions that reflect poignant, telltale, and often tragic choices.

Evil is typically understood in either empirical or metaphysical terms. We know evil either through stark examples that defy explanation or from abstruse theorizing that evades demonstration. Consider the analogy of the Divided Line in Plato's *Republic* (1968). The analogy shows a hierarchical relation between different kinds of knowledge. Below the line, there is first sense-perception and then perception of visual images; above the line, there are conceptual hypotheses and then the laws. For Plato, the analogy for different kinds of knowledge bridges the realm of the sensible and the realm of ideas.

Evil collapses the bridge between empiricism and metaphysics. The Divided Line becomes opaque. Nothing from the realm of the sensible passes to the realm of ideas and nothing from the conceptual into the material. Since evil demolishes the possibility of transcendental understanding, it is necessary to rebuild the bridge that evil destroys in order to understand evil.

In 1992, a fairly healthy and relatively functional society was viciously attacked and sadistically abused. Bosnia, with its traditions of multiculturalism and pluralistic communities, was a model for the other republics in former-Yugoslavia. Tito's notion of "Brotherhood and Unity" was internalized in Bosnia more than in the other Yugoslav republics. Bosnia, though, seemed to digress into what Thomas Hobbes calls a state of war where the situation is all against all. The only cardinal virtues seemed to be force and fraud, and the world abetted this process.

What was the situation in Bosnia? Every day children, women, and unarmed men were murdered. Every week mass murders occurred. Sadistic rape camps were constructed. The motivation behind these war crimes and crimes against humanity was to destroy a community and demolish the social order upon which the community thrived for centuries. Hobbes says that, in fact, the presocial state of nature has never existed. The natural state is too painful to last for any period of time. For Hobbes, the presocial state of nature is simply an ideal type. He simply uses the notion for heuristic purposes—to explain the origins of society.

Bosnia thus confronts us. When we try to grasp the recent history of Bosnia, it is impossible not to raise the subject of evil. In turn, when we seek to comprehend what evil is, it is parochial not to turn our attention to Bosnia. We need Bosnia, her wisdom and traditions of transcendence. In the face of unimaginable suffering, people from Bosnia came to understand the paradoxes of evil. Evil is the attempt to kill the social, to murder action itself. While evil simulates action, it ultimately belies itself as action.

Can someone choose to do evil? Socrates says no. No one willingly does evil. Although this book tries hard to overcome the Socratic point of view, looking for evil's agency, purpose, means, conditions, and, finally, evil's normative orientation, the search fails. At the end, the book accepts the Socratic position. Action, which is evil, is unthinkable.

2. Evil's Direction

Evil is lack of direction, and that which is done in it and out of it is the grasping, seizing, devouring, compelling, seducing, exploiting, humiliating, torturing, and destroying of what offers itself.

—Martin Buber

"Ethnic cleansing" is a widely misused euphemism for the arrests, expulsions, rapes, and murders of Bosnian citizens. The use of this phrase obstructs an adequate understanding of the activity that the term labels. The term is euphemistic because the word "cleansing" implies an activity that is ordinary, harmless, and even beneficial. There, however, was nothing ordinary, harmless, or beneficial about the arrests, expulsions, rapes, and murders of hundreds of thousands of Bosnian citizens.

In 1992, before the war, there were 4.5 million inhabitants of Bosnia. During the war, close to one-quarter of a million were killed, one-quarter of a million injured, and one-quarter of a million held in concentration camps. Over 2 million of Bosnia's inhabitants were forced to abandon their homes to become refugees in another part of their country or another country altogether.

An earlier version of this chapter appeared first as "O latentnoj funkciji etničkog čišćenja u Bosni" in *Forum Bosnae* and then as "On the Latent Function of Ethnic Cleansing in Bosnia" in *Sociology after Bosnia and Kosovo: Recovering Justice.*

The American sociologist Robert K. Merton (1968) argues that as long as functional analysis restricts its focus to the manifest function of social conduct, it remains deficient. According to Merton, in sociology function is determined not by the subjective dispositions of conduct or the rational motivations governing the activity, but by the objective and actual consequences of the conduct itself. Merton theorizes that aims and purposes often have little to do with the objective consequences of social conduct. According to Merton, aims and consequences operate independently of each other; such is the irrationality of social life. Moreover, consequences are often unintended and unrecognized, which is why Merton introduces the concept of latent function. Thus, to understand what truly governs social conduct, it is necessary to address not the conduct's aim but its objective consequences.

In *Bosnia: A Short History*, Noel Malcolm concludes with a commentary on the unconscionable events occuring at the time of the book's publication. His conclusion evokes Merton's sociological distinction between manifest and latent function. Malcolm first writes:

> The pattern was set by young urban gangsters in expensive sunglasses from Serbia, members of the paramilitary forces raised by Arkan and others; and though the individuals who performed these acts may have gained some pathological pleasure from them, what they were doing was to carry out a rational strategy dictated by their political leaders—a method carefully calculated to drive out two ethnic populations and radicalize a third. (1994, 252)

The overt purpose of ethnic cleansing, its manifest function, was to drive out the Bosnian Croats and Bosnian Muslims from their homes and communities and to radicalize the Bosnian Serbs.

Malcolm, then, identifies another understanding of why ethnic cleansing was occurring, citing the historian Richard Pipes on a different period. This passage concludes Malcolm's book:

> But perhaps the best comment on the tactic of Milošević and Mladić and on what they have achieved in Bosnia . . . is a judgment by another historian on another country's descent into blood. . . . "The Bolsheviks had to spill blood in order to bind their waving adherents with a band of collective guilt. The more innocent victims the Bolshevik Party had on its conscience, the

more the Bolshevik rank and file had to realize there was no retreating, no faltering, no compromising, that they were inextricably bound to their leaders, and could only march with them to 'total victory' regardless of the cost." (1994, 252)

The latent function of ethnic cleansing was "to spill blood in order to bind" Bosnian Serbs together with a band of collective guilt. Its objective consequence was to replace the social solidarity that Bosnian Serbs had with other Bosnians with a social solidarity based on nationalism and prejudice.

Ethnic cleansing took on its most abusive form in Bosnia not because there is a long-standing history of tribal hatred in Bosnia, but because there is a long-standing history of tolerance and openness in Bosnia. There is a well-documented history of respect toward different customs and traditions among Bosnians. There is a compelling legacy of goodwill toward guests and people from different ethnicities. Given the normative orientations that supported social order throughout Bosnia's history and that were admired throughout former-Yugoslavia, ethnic cleansing had to be done in ways that were categorical. Ethnic cleansing had to be done in ways that were ruthless and absolute. Since the social relations of Bosnian Serbs with their neighbors were long-standing and profound, much blood needed to be spilled in order to sever these relations.

Consider these passages on the pathos of ethnic cleansing from three distinguished works on the war: Michael A. Sells's (1996) *The Bridge Betrayed: Religion and Genocide in Bosnia*, Peter Maass's (1997) *Love Thy Neighbor: A Story of War*, and David Rohde's (1997) *Endgame: The Betrayal and Fall of Srebrenica: Europe's Worst Massacre since World War II*. First, Sells shares this report:

> Serbs who refused to participate in the persecution of Muslims were killed. In a Serb-army occupied area of Sarajevo, Serb militants killed a Serb officer who objected to atrocities against civilians; they left his body on the street for over a week as an object lesson. During one of the "selections" carried out by Serb militants in Sarajevo, an old Serb named Ljubo objected to being separated out from his Muslim friends and neighbors; they beat him to death on the spot. In Zvornik, Serb militiamen slit the throat of a seventeen-year-old Serb girl who protested the shooting of Muslim civilians. In the Prijedor region, Serb militants put Serbs

accused of helping non-Serb neighbors into the camps with those they tried to help. (1996, 73)

Sells then brings our attention to the following practice:

> Commanders of the killing camps made a practice of opening them to local Serb radicals, gangsters, and grudge-holders, who would come each night to beat, torture, and kill the detainees. This practice had the effect of spreading complicity throughout the neighboring area. Distribution of stolen and abandoned goods also spread complicity. Every town "cleansed" meant the availability of automobiles, appliances, stereo and television equipment. Once a family had in their home something that had belonged to a neighbor, they were less likely to object to the "ethnic cleansing." (1996, 74)

Next, in *Love Thy Neighbor* Maass theorizes the political pathos guiding ethnic cleansing.

> Gaining the support of ordinary people . . . is a crucial element of any successful reign of terror. The wavering masses, the silent majority, the good men, they must feel stained by the same blood as the Visigoths who fired the first shots. They must be made into accomplices to the crime. Once this is done, once their moral backs are broken, they will do virtually anything. Like Želja [a sniper in the hills of Sarajevo] they will even fire shots that might kill their own parents [Želja's parents lived in Sarajevo during its siege]. (1997, 112)

Finally, in *Endgame*, Rohde chronicles the fall of Srebrenica from the viewpoint of those who suffered the atrocity, as well as those who committed it. Reporting an anecdote from Dražen Erdemović, an executioner during the Srebrenica massacre, Rohde notes the following account from Erdemović's testimony: "Before the last group were executed, Gojković [the squad's commander] entered the bus and handed a Kalashnikov to the driver. 'You must each kill one,' he said to the horrified driver. He didn't want anyone talking. Everyone would be guilty" (1997, 309).

During the fall of Srebrenica, not only were individuals co-opted into the conduct of ethnic cleansing, but entire villages were implicated as well. Consider the ritual by which Bosnian Muslim men, who were retained in Bratunac, a Serb-held town northeast of Srebrenica, were executed:

> [Six hundred] Muslim prisoners who had sweltered through Mladić's speech on the Nova Kasaba soccer field were packed shoulder to shoulder in two sixty-foot-long, sixteen-wheel trucks. . . . For three hours, the men stood in the stifling trucks. At 11 P.M., guards finally lifted the top off the back entrance of the truck. Local Serb men and women from Bratunac were waiting. They asked if any Muslims from Bratunac or any old friends they knew were on board. "We brought you dinner," they said, or "We brought you cigarettes." About twenty Muslims got off the truck. They were asked questions briefly and then the Serbs began to beat them. The men in the truck listened to their cries, and then heard pistol fire. None of the twenty returned.
>
> At 12:30 A.M., more people appeared at the back of Hodžić's truck, wanting to know if there were any Muslims from the villages of Kravica and Lolići on the truck. About twenty Muslim men, either deciding that they wanted to die or believing somehow that their friends would spare them, got off. They were immediately beaten. "Fuck your Gypsy mother!" one Serb shouted. Again, shots were heard. Again, none of the twenty returned. (Rohde 1997, 281–82)

The evil of ethnic cleansing was to disfigure the normative orientations to which Bosnian Serbs and others were historically subject as members of Bosnian society. The objective consequence was to maim the collective sentiments that integrated Bosnians in their society and guided them in their interactions with others. The result was to detach Bosnians from the value elements they had used to make judgments not only about others, but also about themselves.

The criminal sentiments and evil behavior of Serbian nationalist leaders created the mind-set of a crowd. Gustave Le Bon says that, while a crowd is a social phenomenon, a crowd lacks the structure of a society. As a social entity, a crowd remains a deficient society. Le Bon, however, notes that sometimes "an entire nation may become a crowd under the action of certain influences" (1982, 3). This is what happened in Serbia under Slobodan Milošević and what spread to neighboring countries. The normative orientation with which the Bosnian Serbs engaged in ethnic cleansing was the delusional mind of a crowd. Drawing upon a passage from *Catch-22*, Maass provides a caricature of this crowd mentality that overtook not only nationalist Bosnian Serbs, but also, with the passing of time, other ethnic communities.

> Everyone knew that sin was evil and that no good could come from evil. But . . . it was almost no trick at all . . . to turn vice into virtue, and slander into truth, impotence into abstinence, arrogance into humility, plunder into philanthropy, thievery into honor, blasphemy into wisdom, brutality into patriotism, and sadism into justice. Anybody could do it; it required no brains at all. It merely required no character. (1996, 209)

Western leaders and United Nations officials had detailed reports of the perverse manner and sadistic degree to which ethnic cleansing was occurring. While they had adequate descriptions of what was happening, Western leaders and UN officials lacked an objective understanding of why it was occurring. They accepted the seemingly rational accounts provided by the actors planning, promoting, and inciting ethnic cleansing. They accepted that the aim, purpose, and goal of ethnic cleansing was to drive apart two ethnic populations in Bosnia and radicalize a third. The goal of creating a nation-state with a homogeneous population was accepted as justifying the means employed. Western leaders and UN officials granted the rationality of ethnic cleansers too much significance and failed to recognize what the objective consequences of ethnic cleansing were. They were seduced by the utilitarian rationality of the ethnic cleansers in part because this type of rationality implicitly controlled the conduct of Western leaders and UN officials themselves.

The conscious aim behind ethnic cleansing, however, failed to explain why this conduct was necessary from the viewpoint of the actors engaged in ethnic cleansing. The manifest function, that is, the need to drive apart two ethnic populations and to radicalize a third, is insufficient to explain what compelled and sustained the gruesome conduct from 1992 to 1995. From the viewpoint of the Bosnian Serbs who saw themselves as Bosnian, there was no need for ethnic cleansing. From the viewpoint of the Bosnian Serbs who saw themselves as Yugoslavs, there was no purpose for ethnic cleansing. From the viewpoint of the Bosnian Serbs whose spouses and relatives were non-Serbs, there was no desire for ethnic cleansing.

While the manifest function of ethnic cleansing was to drive apart two ethnic populations and radicalize a third, this rationalization does not adequately explain why the conduct occurred. The manifest function for ethnic cleansing is not even as rational as it purports. Bosnia was partitioned, tragically fractured. The end of ethnic cleansing can be said to have been achieved. The signing of the Dayton Peace Accord accepted and endorsed the objective consequence of ethnic cleansing with the creation of Republika Srpska, a hostile ministate within the federation of Bosnia-Herzegovina. If the end of ethnic cleansing was tacitly achieved and even sanctioned by world leaders with the signing of the Dayton Accord, why would the pathos of activity still be present? What function did the activity really serve?

The latent function of ethnic cleansing grew in significance in part because it was not recognized. As the significance of the latent function of ethnic cleansing increased, the activity intensified. The need on the part of those engaged in ethnic cleansing to gain the complicity of not only Bosnian Serbs but also the leaders of Western nations became overwhelming. In accepting at face value the manifest purpose of ethnic cleansing and in pandering to the leaders who brazenly promoted this purpose, Western leaders and UN officials become implicated in the same manner as Bosnian Serbs. To give one example, the manifest function for the fall of Srebrenica and Žepa, two UN-designated safe havens, was to make negotiations possible and complete the seemingly inevitable process of partition. UN officials openly rationalized this position with world leaders (Jagger 1995). The latent function of the fall of Srebrenica and Žepa, however, was to humiliate Western leaders and UN officials, and this determined the activity to a far greater degree than the manifest function. The latent function of the fall of Srebrenica and Žepa, from the viewpoint of those who planned and carried out the atrocity, was to show that the moral integrity of Western leaders and UN officials was no different than that of the nationalist Serb leaders.

Western leaders and UN officials did not understand why, after being exposed in the world media with outstanding journalism, ethnic cleansing not only persisted but also intensified. They did not understand why exposure increased rather than diminished the excesses of ethnic cleansing. Nor did they understand the barely hidden logic that fueled ethnic cleansing. They did not recognize the need on the part of national Serb leaders to win the endorsement and tacit approval of Western leaders and UN officials for the hideous process misleadingly labeled ethnic cleansing. Although Western leaders and UN officials verbally and bombastically condemned ethnic cleansing, they accepted it behaviorally and tacitly.

The sociologist Charles Horton Cooley makes the following point about human nature and its place in society:

> Human nature in this sense is justly regarded as a comparatively permanent element in society. Always and everywhere men seek honor and dread ridicule, defer to public opinion, cherish their goods and their children, and admire courage, generosity, and success. (1962, 30–31)

Did those engaged in ethnic cleansing exemplify an absence of human nature? They sought honor, albeit in perverse ways. They also dreaded ridicule. Western leaders and UN officials assumed that human nature was utterly absent in the conduct of ethnic cleansing. How could human beings, they reasoned, do the horrific things that these perpetrators did? It was not understood how human nature, in fact, remained a permanent element of society even when human nature sought to destroy the society upon which it depended. Western leaders and UN officials did not see how human nature resented the failure of society to confront its own self-destructiveness. If human nature were understood and therefore recognized as a permanent element of society, Western leaders and UN officials would have known better how to employ this notion and confront the human nature engaged in the destruction of its social world. They would have recognized that it is possible for evil to be shamed and that herein lies the way to effectively confront evil.

Instead, Western leaders and UN officials embraced the position articulated by Lance Morrow in *Evil: An Investigation*: "It is difficult to make evil ashamed of itself. I am not sure it can be done. Not with true shame, surely, which implies a remnant decency" (2002, 69). Western leaders and UN officials failed to recognize the falseness of this assumption and did not consider the more rational and humane alternative. The vanity that fueled the evil of ethnic cleansing was a point of weakness and an instance of vulnerability. Shame is knowledge of one's thoughtlessness. If evil is nothing more than thoughtlessness, shame is the awareness of this state. Shame is always a possibility insofar as human nature is indeed a permanent element of society.

3. Evil's Reason

> The fact that the concept of evil has no explanatory power just
> when we feel most need of it does not mean that it is inessential
> to our understanding of what happens even then.
> —Raimond Gaita

What is the evil in war crimes? The word "evil" is a signifier, and its meaning needs to be recovered; otherwise, the word loses its significance despite the preponderance of its use. During the war against Bosnia, the nationalist Serb Army and the Yugoslav People's Army deliberately targeted civilian funerals. Massacres sometimes occurred during services, thus preventing family members from burying their loved ones. Communities were forced to abandon their deceased in fields or on streets. The war criminals then grotesquely discarded the bodies into remote pits or inaccessible mines. Sometimes they planted grenades into these pits to discourage the recovery of the bodies.

The term "mass graves" is a misnomer because mass graves are not graves. Religious ceremonies and social rituals were not properly performed. While saying prayers for the dead, religious leaders took refuge from shelling by jumping into graves. In Sarajevo, Serbian snipers attacked and killed those preparing graves. Women and children were deliberately wounded or killed by shells while throwing dirt into a grave during a service.

An earlier version of this chapter was presented at the Institute for Research of Crimes against Humanity and International Law in Bihać, Bosnia, Septem-

To address the question of the evil in war crimes, it helps first to review the social ritual that was violated and transgressed by revisiting some of the important social science literature on the subject. In modern times, the significance of the burial ceremony may be taken for granted or treated indifferently. The failure of the world to recognize the evil in the attacks on the funeral and the prevention of burial reflects a modern sensibility that neglects to recognize the significance of the burial.

Since the dawn of society, human burials have existed. Even if today men and women do not ponder the meaning of the ritual, as long as there is a society, even an atheistic society, the ritual still exists. This chapter addresses two interrelated questions: What is the meaningfulness of the funeral ceremony and what does it mean to transgress this inviolable ritual? The anthropologist Clyde Kluckhohn defines a funeral as "a symbolic assertion that a person is important not only to his immediate relatives but to the whole group" (1964, 136). The funeral is essentially a ritual, and a ritual is a collective symbolic assertion. However the rite may be conducted, funerals are symbolic rituals with distinctive cultural patterns regardless of religious practice or lack thereof.

The video documentary *The Siege of Sarajevo: 1992–1996* by FAMA Associates chronicles the lives and experiences of people from various walks of life. In one testimony, Vlado Raguž, director of the Funeral Services Company of Sarajevo, explains how formidable it was to provide funerals for the dead. Since coffins were not available, wooden wardrobes were used instead. To transport the deceased from their homes to the mortuary and to the cemetery, petrol had to be purchased from black marketers at thirty Deutsche Marks a liter. Nevertheless, under impossible circumstances, fifteen thousand people were buried during the siege with ceremonies. The community and people of Sarajevo account for this inadequately recognized achievement. During the siege, the community fought desperately to retain its ethical and human character despite the most vicious circumstances and despite the world's unconscionable betrayal of the city.

Sociologist Émile Durkheim says, "It is no longer out of affection that we mourn the dead, it is out of duty" (1975, 15). Emotional trauma

---

ber 2000, and then published as "What Is the Evil of War Crimes? The Ethical Requirement of Burial and Its Transgression in the War Bosnia-Herzegovina" in *Peace, Conflict, and Development*.

and psychological instability are components of the human burial. The funeral provides comfort during times of great emotional distress and reassures the community of continuity after suffering a profound loss. However, ultimately it is duty that makes the burial rite necessary; the funeral exemplifies the innate ethical spirit of the human species. This duty is the moral lifeblood of society.

Throughout the war, the global media depicted conditions in Bosnia as analogous to a Hobbesian jungle; it indicated that the only cardinal virtues in Bosnia were force and fraud. The popular story line was "Might is right" and "Every man for himself." Ethical duty, it seemed, was absent within the subject.

Sarajevo, however, did not digress into a presocial state of "a war of all against all." The fact that fifteen thousand people were provided funeral services under utterly inhumane and impossibly dangerous conditions supports this argument. The ethical spirit of the community persevered, and the social fabric of the community was not shredded, despite every effort to do so. The community remained intact.

Human burials have empirical and theological significance. Empirically, they serve as the evolutionary marker for the birth of human nature (Solecki 1971). Human burials exemplify recognition of the distinctiveness of the human species in relation to other species. The burial is the first meaningful ritual in the evolution of the human species; the ritual defines the human species as what it is. Herein lies the ethical content of the burial. The burial, not death, defines what human beings are.

In performing the burial rite, human beings are not merely conscious of their life-activity; they are self-conscious, and this self-consciousness distinguishes the human species from other species. Unlike animals, humans are not immediately one with their life-activity; they make their life-activity an objective of reflection (Marx 2004). During the burial ceremony, the life-activity of the individual and the community in relation to the individual become the object of reflection. In the face of death, human beings are impelled to take special action.

The burial ritual symbolically represents the self-consciousness of human beings at a collective level. On this point, the anthropologist A. L. Kroeber writes

> When prehistoric skeletons are found in the position in which death might take place, the presumption is that the people of that

time abandoned their dead as animals would. If, on the other hand, a skeleton lies intact with its arms carefully folded, there is little room for doubt human beings had arrived at a crude recognition of the difference between flesh and spirit. (1923, 171)

Human beings are not able to ignore the cessation of activity and the lapse of consciousness that accompany death. Human beings are impelled to take special action. Kroeber theorizes, "Even to say that Neanderthal man did not know whether his dead were dead implies his recognition of something different from life in the body, for he recognized of course that the body had become different" (1923, 171).

For this reason, the disposal of the corpse has never been a matter of expedience or practical function. Kluckhohn writes, "It is truly amazing that no known group has ever adopted the functionally simplest mode of disposing of its dead—merely abandoning corpses or disposing of them without a rite of any sort" (1964, 134). The very phrase, "disposal of the corpse," belies the symbolic action that accompanies burial. While the burial is performed with varying degrees of cultural complexity and religious concerns, there is always a ritual whose symbolic content shows dignity and respect for the individual, as well as the human species of which the individual is a part.

In *The Phenomenology of Mind*, G. W. F. Hegel formulates the tension between the empirical and the theological understanding of the burial ritual, and in a dialectical manner he reconciles their tension. With the burial service, the right of consciousness asserts itself over and against nature. With the prayer, "You are dust and to dust you shall return," the right of nature over human flesh is granted. At the same time, the funeral prayer denies nature its right to subsume the person entirely. By its special action, the rite denies nature its right to subsume the spirit of the person. "You are dust and to dust you shall return" lifts the spirit of the person out of the clutches of nature even as it grants nature its claim to the body of the deceased. Hegel writes lucidly on this ethical spirit, an ethical spirit expressed distinctively in every culture and in every historical period.

> The family keeps away from the dead this dishonoring of him by the desires of unconscious organic agencies and by abstract elements, puts its own action in place of theirs, and weds the relative to the bosom of the earth, the elemental individuality that passes

not away. Thereby the family makes the dead a member of a community which prevails over and holds under control the powers of the particular material elements and the lower living creatures, which sought to have their way with the dead and destroy him. (1977, 472)

What then does it mean to transgress the burial ritual? What does it mean to transgress the burial ritual violently and sadistically? In the video documentary *We Are All Neighbors* with Tone Bringa, there is this report from a refugee within her own country.

"All slaughtered. No one was left alive. They set fire to everything that was good in our lives. Everything destroyed . . . everyone slaughtered and killed. They didn't allow us to bury the dead. They were left."

"Not allowed to bury the dead?"

"No. Some tried to bury their relatives but they could not. Three days they tried, got wounded, but they wouldn't let them. So the bodies decomposed in the streets and in the fields. That's how it is."

This horrendous experience occurred too frequently during the war in Bosnia; it occurred so frequently that it has been neither adequately reported nor adequately addressed. The deed described is odious. Evil is not an abstract concept. The crime against humanity that the refugee reports is not merely a matter of preventing her and her family from burying their dead; the crime is forcing her family to abandon their dead despite the family making every effort and taking every risk to do otherwise. Duty requires the family to provide a burial for their dead, and this duty is immutable even if it puts them in harm's way.

The exercise of this duty represents the ethical spirit of the human species, something innate in every family. If the family is unable to perform this duty, a sense of remorse arises. No matter how blameless the family is, if a funeral ceremony for a loved one does not occur, there is a profound feeling of regret. This remorse does not reflect the absence of the ethical spirit in the family, but rather its presence. The deeper the ethical spirit is within the family, the deeper the remorse if the family is unable to bury a loved one. The evil of crimes against humanity is that they strike at the foundation of society.

In *Magic, Science, and Religion,* the anthropologist Bronislaw Malinowski makes this point: "In the tending of the corpse . . . the nearest relatives . . . always show horror and fear mingled with pious love, but never do the negative elements appear alone or even dominate" (1954, 48). With the burial ritual, the negative elements of fear and horror appear, but not alone. Neither do the negative elements dominate. With the burial ritual, the negative elements are countered by the positive element of pious love. In *The Elementary Forms of Religious Life*, Durkheim (1915, 414) says "it is because rites serve to remake individuals and groups morally that they are believed to have a power over things," and this point reinforces the argument. The evil that occurred in Bosnia was not only the murdering of countless civilians; it was also the attempt to create a strictly negative response, a response only of horror and fear, to death within the family and the community. The evil was also to insist that the negative elements alone dominate. The evil was the attempt to destroy the family by violating the inviolate duty of the family. If a family believes it has forsaken its ethical duty to its loved ones, the family has trouble recovering from its victimization. Through no fault of its own, the family lapses into fear for its very being. Evil makes it difficult for families to continue as families, no matter where they come to be located after suffering such violence. Despite a family's forced relocation, its duty to lost loved ones does not go away.

The video documentary *A Cry from the Grave* depicts this issue starkly. The documentary focuses on the plight of women from Srebrenica who lost their sons, brothers, husbands, and grandfathers during the genocide. Today there is a pressing need for the survivors to identify the remains of the deceased recovered from mass graves, and it is helpful to recognize the weighty reason for the immense labor that goes into meeting this need. Identification is vital in order to allow for the possibility of burial. If identification of the body has not taken place, it is difficult to hold an adequate funeral. The ethical spirit of the family is stymied because it yearns to perform its duty for the dead, but it cannot if the remains of the deceased are not first identified. The longer it takes to recover the human remains, the less likely identification is possible. The longer identification takes, the harder it is to perform the necessary burial.

In *The Fate of the Earth*, Jonathan Schell writes, "Evil becomes radical whenever it goes beyond destroying individual victims (in whatever numbers) and, in addition, mutilates or destroys the *world* that can in some way respond to—and thus in some measure redeem—the deaths suffered" (1982, 145). What were the nationalist Serb Army and the Yugoslav People's Army doing when they shelled civilian funerals? What were the war criminals doing when they disposed of murdered bodies in mines and pits? It is crucial to ask these questions. Evil becomes radical when it goes beyond the evil of destroying individuals. Evil seeks to mutilate the lifeworld that can in some way respond to the deaths suffered; it seeks to destroy not only the individuals but also the family as a social unit. Moreover, if the ethical spirit of the family is destroyed, then so is the community in which the family resides.

In making it impossible to identify the remains from mass graves, the victims are twice abused. Schell explains, "It lays a special obligation on the people of the future to deal with the crime, even long after its perpetrators are themselves dead" (1982, 161). Genocide describes only in part the activity and consequences of "ethnic cleansing." As powerful as the term is, genocide may not fully encompass what ethnic cleansing was. The heinous acts were not just genocide but also sociocide. One reason for the confusion as to what was happening in Bosnia during the war is that the differences between genocide and sociocide were played off each other. Genocide and sociocide are two words signifying two different things. Schell helps us understand what is particular about sociocide: "When crimes are of a certain magnitude and character, they nullify our power to respond to them adequately because they smash the human context in which human losses normally acquire their meaning for us" (1982, 145). Society is the human context in which human losses acquire their meaning for us; to murder this context is to destroy, not just an ethnic group or particular community of people, but a society itself.

Why was the violence brought to bear in this particular way against the people and communities of Bosnia? The enemies of Bosnia were striking at the heart of her society; they were seeking to destroy the vitality and the backbone of Bosnia's community. Can this be? Can a society truly be murdered? Is this what evil is? Although it seems possible to murder society, and some may argue that such has happened at various times in history, society may, in fact, have a kind of immortal character. The human species has an unfathomable resilience. This resiliency is exemplified in the social world. Not every element of society, in other words, is empirical. Elements that are nonempirical gather society. Evil makes us forget this truth. The reason why it is impossible to kill society resides not in the empirical itself. Comments from Malinowski help affirm this point:

> We have seen already how religion, by sacralizing and thus standardizing the other set of impulses, bestows on man the gift of mental integrity. . . . In all this religion counteracts the centrifugal forces of fear, dismay, demoralization, and provides the most powerful means of reintegration of the group's shaken solidarity and of the re-establishment of its morale. . . . Religion here assures the victory of tradition and culture over the mere negative response of thwarted instinct. (1954, 53)

The people of Bosnia survived an unconscionable war and an unfathomable betrayal, and most survived it with the gift of integrity. Their community remained intact, albeit deeply severed. Many journalists working in Bosnia during the war witnessed and reported this gift of mental integrity, a gift inherited from the different religious traditions and cultural customs of Bosnia. It would be wrong to say that, during the war, the world saw only the fearful and horrific elements of death. While the world indeed saw these elements, it also witnessed what Malinowski refers to as the gift of mental integrity in the deeds of Bosnians, particularly in her everyday citizens. The world admired this integrity that Bosnians, drawing upon their rich social and cultural inheritances, exemplified. For an anthology of poignant testimonials demonstrating this point, see Svetlana Broz's *Good People in an Evil Time* (2004).

The world also lamented the frequent absence of the gift of mental integrity among the political leaders responding to the evil in Bosnia. Bosnia was attacked because of what it was—a pluralistic, integrated, inclusive society. A nation-state with a shallow, one-dimensional sense of solidarity could not be established in either Serbia or Croatia when a superior model of solidarity based on pluralism and inclusiveness existed on its borders. When Serbia and Croatia were established as homogeneous nation-states that glorified one dominant ethnicity, the social character of Bosnia, which belied the nationalist ideologies of her neighbors, became a threat. For the nationalistic leaders of the newly created nation-states of Serbia and Croatia, this threat at their borders needed to be destroyed. Bosnia, however, survived the attack because of what it had been and will continue to be—a society that reflects a multiconfessional community with syncretistically infused traditions.

It is important for people in other countries to remember their own tragedies in order to empathize with the situation that Bosnians suffer.

For example, the POW-MIA movement in the United States remains an emotional one. Although it has been years since the Vietnam War ended, families still want the remains of their sons and fathers returned to the United States from Vietnam. The underlying issue for Americans is the same as it is for Bosnians. The issue is the duty of families to bury their sons and fathers who died in a war and the responsibility of the U.S. government to assist families in this regard. The tenacity of the issue for Americans reflects the ethical spirit of the American families who lost sons and fathers in Vietnam and the sensitivity of society toward this ethical spirit. The POW-MIA movement, even after thirty years, remains a political one; POW-MIA flags are still displayed in parades and at post offices throughout the United States. The issue is not whether the Vietnam War was right or wrong: the issue is the inviolable right of the family to exercise its duty. This right is not only based on a family's affection for the lost member; it is also based on the family's ethical duty and its undying responsibility to perform this duty. The duty represents the self-consciousness of the family as a part of humanity and the desire of the family to preserve its innate nature.

Consider also one surprising confrontation that happened shortly after September 11, 2001. New York City firemen were unwilling to give up their search for lost colleagues after the destruction of the World Trade Center. The confrontation that occurred between New York City firemen, who wanted to continue to search for lost colleagues, and New York City police, who wanted to stop the search for dead bodies at the site of the tragedy, indicates how powerful the duty to bury lost ones is. This response of the New York City firemen to the tragedy of 9/11 and then their confrontation with the New York City police can be used to predict how the tragedies in Bosnia will not disappear with the passing of time. The right of family to assert itself over and against the forces of nature that subsume the remains of a family member does not fade with time. Understanding and addressing this issue sociologically and politically is imperative to restoring a lasting peace in Bosnia.

4. Evil's Vanity

> What protects us is that in nuclear war the event is likely to eliminate the possibility of the spectacle. *This is why it will not take place.* For humanity can accept physical annihilation, but cannot accept to sacrifice the spectacle (unless it can find a spectator in another world). The drive to spectacle is more powerful than the instinct of preservation, and it is on the former that we must rely.
>
> —Jean Baudrillard

While it is easy to identify the political motive behind ethnic cleansing, it is more difficult to understand the social motive. The costs were too high not only for the victims, but also for the victimizers. The perpetrators destroyed not only the homes, the communities, and the lives of people who had been neighbors, but also the social fabric and cultural conventions upon which they, too, had depended. In the video documentary *Killing Memory: Bosnia's Cultural Heritage and Its Destruction*, produced by the Community of Bosnia Foundation, Andras Reidlmayer says that ethnic cleansing was an assault not just against people and their lives, but also against the historical buildings and cultural monuments of Bosnia:

Earlier versions of this chapter were presented as "The Ritual of Shame and the Western Response to Bosnia" at the Bosnian Paradigm International Conference, Sarajevo, Bosnia, November 1998, and published in *Sociology after Bosnia and Kosovo: Recovering Bosnia* and as "Evil and the Ritual of Shame: A Crime against Humanity in Bosnia-Herzegovina" in *Janus Head*.

When a person dies, it is that person's life, that person's family that's affected. When a culture is killed, it forecloses the future and it destroys the memory of the past. Even if the people to whom those monuments and documents belong survive, they've lost their anchor, their connection to who they are, of how they belong to a particular place. . . . I think that you cannot separate the sufferings of people from the destruction of monuments of culture. The killing of memory is as great a tragedy as the killing of people.

Harold Garfinkel published a short essay in the *American Journal of Sociology* titled "Conditions of Successful Degradation Ceremonies." Degradation ceremonies, Garfinkel says, are "any communicative work between persons, whereby the public identity of an actor is transformed into something looked on as lower in the local scheme of social types" (1956, 420). Ethnic cleansing is a degradation ceremony. With sadistic violence and unconscionable aggression, ethnic cleansers attempted to transform the public identities of individuals and a community. Nationalist Serbs sought to transform the social identities of Bosnian Muslims into something looked upon as lower in the local scheme of social types. First, this activity occurred in the state media and intellectual circles. Then, militia, with the support of the Yugoslav People's Army, entered Bosnia and methodically engaged in horrendous activities.

In his book *Love Thy Neighbor: A Story of War*, Peter Maass reports a painful event, one that is representative of the sadistic way in which ethnic cleansing was carried out:

> You can, for example, barge into a house and put a gun to a father's head and tell him that you will pull the trigger unless he rapes his daughter or at least simulates rape. (I heard of such things in Bosnia.) The father will refuse and say, I will die before doing that. You shrug your shoulders and reply, Okay, old man, I won't shoot you, but I will shoot your daughter. What does the father do now, dear reader? He pleads, he begs, but then you, the man with the gun, put the gun to the daughter's head, you pull back the hammer, and you shout, Now! Do it! Or I shoot! The father starts weeping, yet slowly he unties his belt, moving like a dazed zombie, he can't believe what he must do. You laugh and say, That's right, old man, pull down those pants, pull up your daughter's dress, and do it! (1997, 51–52)

In narrating the pathos of this event, Maass employs the second-person pronoun, "you." To win the reader's indignation, Maass puts the reader in the place of the gunman, assuming that the reader will be repulsed. Yes, the reader will seek distance from the activity of the gunman, but, by default, the reader will also seek distance from the gunman's victims. To counter this possibility, the following discussion reassigns the reference and uses the second-person pronoun to refer to the father, drawing readers closer to the father.

If the gunman tells you that he will kill your daughter unless you have sexual intercourse with her and if you know that the gunman is capable of murdering a human being, how can you not comply? You state first that you will die before you do what the gunman asks. The gunman responds that, unless you do what he asks, he will kill your daughter. For the sake of your dignity, you are willing to sacrifice your life, but it is not your life that the gunman wants—it is your dignity.

You comply, but what is the nature of your compliance? You comply because you are a father. The gunman's conduct, in other words, does not transform you into a nonfather. Your dignity, the first principle of what it is to be a father, is left untouched because the ultimate grounds for your conduct are clear. You cherish the life of your daughter; you cannot bear to watch her murdered. While, for the sake of your dignity, you are willing to sacrifice your life, you are not, for the sake of your dignity, willing to sacrifice your daughter's life. Your daughter's life is more important to you than your dignity. If you had sacrificed your daughter's life for the sake of your dignity, you would have lost your dignity. You would have ceased to be a father.

The gunman has power over you not because of his gun. The gun alone signifies no power at all. Wherein then lies the gunman's power over you? One aspect of the gunman's power is the absence of any normative constraint regarding his use of force. Another and more important aspect of his power is your need to not witness your daughter being murdered. Your need makes you dependent on the gunman. The gunman has power over you because you cherish your daughter. The gunman recognizes your need and the dependence on him it creates. Neither the gun nor the gunman's anomic use of the gun explains his power over you. It is rather your need to not see your daughter murdered and your steadfast relation to this need that explains the gunman's power.

The gunman seeks to degrade you. Here is the aim that governs his behavior and the pathos of ethnic cleansing. The better we understand this pathos, the better we are able to understand the evil of ethnic cleansing. The better we understand the evil of ethnic cleansing, the better we are able to redress its consequences.

For a status degradation ceremony to be successful, "the identities referred to," Garfinkel says, "must be 'total' identities. That is, these identities must refer to persons as 'motivational' types rather than as 'behavioral' types, not to what a person may be expected to have done or to do . . . but to what the group holds to be the ultimate 'grounds' or 'reasons' for his performance." In other words, "the transformation of identities," Garfinkel continues, "is the destruction of one social object and the constitution of another. . . . It is not that the old object has been overhauled; rather it is replaced by another. One declares, 'Now, it was otherwise in the first place'" (1956, 421–22). Victimizers would call their victims pejorative names before the occurrence of violence. The victims' identity as Yugoslav citizens within a pluralistic society was replaced with fascist and derogatory labels that were falsely stipulated. Before raping or murdering their victim, ethnic cleansers would bear false witness against the one being victimized. They first sought to transform the identity of their victims in a radical way. As Garfinkel indicates, it was not just a matter of the old identity being overhauled but rather replaced with another.

In the earlier example, the gunman wants to debase you. Does the activity, however, say anything substantive about you as a father, about the ultimate grounds or reasons for your conduct? Does the event, orchestrated by the gunman, touch upon either you or your daughter's "total identity"? Does the gunman really perform what Garfinkel calls a status degradation ceremony?

Notice the assumptions that the gunman must make to gain whatever perverse pleasure he does from his activity. First, the gunman must assume that you are willing to do whatever you can to save your daughter's life. Second, the gunman must assume that you abhor the idea of raping your daughter. Third, and most important, the gunman must recognize you as a father. Without this recognition with respect to your integrity, the gunman's conduct is unintelligible.

The gunman knows you, not in a particular way, but in a general way. He knows that you are a father, and he knows what it means to be a father. In other words, there is a "We-relation" between the gunman and you. If there were not this "We-relation," the possibility of an attempted degradation ceremony would not be present (Schultz 1955, 543). However, it is painful to acknowledge this We-relation between the gunman and you because the substance of it is nothing except the gunman's negation of the We-relation. The bad faith of the gunman is to perpetuate the We-relation through sheer negativity.

Recall the two conditions present for the gunman to attempt a degradation ceremony. The gunman sees two things. One, you are willing to do whatever you can to save your daughter's life. Two, you abhor the idea of intercourse with your daughter. Without these dual assumptions, the gunman lacks the resources with which to attempt to shame you. Because you are a father, you must do what he says. Because you are a father, you must not do what he says. This is the demented logic that guides the gunman's activity.

Notice that, if your normative expectations were not real and the ultimate principles that ground your conduct were not authentic, the conditions for a status degradation ceremony would be absent. Moreover, if the gunman himself did not recognize the genuineness of your normative orientations, not only to you, but also to your society, he would lack the resources with which to attempt a degradation ceremony.

The nature of evil is not simply its unintelligibility. Innocence imagines that evil is unintelligible. If evil makes no sense, it does not exist. If evil does not exist, it does not have to be recognized. Evil, in fact, exemplifies a parasitic relation to what is intelligible, what makes sense, and what *is*. Evil's host is the social. When the host ignores evil's parasitic relation to it, the host suffers and becomes enervated.

"It is proposed," Garfinkel writes, "that only in societies that are completely demoralized, will an observer be unable to find such ceremonies, since only in total anomie are the conditions of degradation ceremonies lacking" (1956, 420). An opinion frequently stated by pundits and journalists is that the situation in Bosnia was one of total anomie, a place where self-interest and self-interest alone ruled, the reification for four long years of the Hobbesian jungle. Hobbes, though, argues that this presocial state of nature never existed in time and never will. For Hobbes (1968), the presocial state is an ideal type because Hobbes reasons that the Hobbesian jungle is too painful—too nasty and brutish—to last for any period at all. Hobbes uses the concept of a presocial state for heuristic purposes, to explain the origins of society.

Descriptively the Hobbesian account of Bosnia seems accurate, but if it were true, the conditions for degradation ceremonies would be lacking and observers would be unable to witness them. Degradation ceremonies, however, were witnessed; they were witnessed repeatedly and clearly in the media and in journalistic reports. They occurred between civilians, soldiers, political leaders, and foreign diplomats. Although each was distinct, they shared a common pattern. The world was gripped by the thread of these stories and fixated to the ritual they dramatized.

Rather than stipulate that the situation in Bosnia was one of total anomie, a better tack to take is to ask what conditions were present that allowed degradation ceremonies to be observed. What features in the organization of the society prevailed that degradation ceremonies were attempted in seemingly anomic situations? The more ethnic cleaning persisted, the more it became a ritual. The more of a ritual it became, the more it persisted. Moreover, the substance of the ritual was neither political nor psychological. This is why politicians found it difficult to stop the activity and why psychologists found it difficult to diagnose the activity. Ethnic cleansing fueled itself independently of political and psychological motives. The ritual was evil in that it fed parasitically on the existing social structure and its innate intersubjectivity. In terms of the factual social order, there was anomie. In terms of the normative social order, there was not anomie.

The mere presence of these social conditions, however, does not guarantee the success of a degradation ceremony; certain strategies and communicative tactics must be followed. If the criteria are not adequately met, the degradation ceremony fails. At this point, Garfinkel introduces the role of the witness in the status degradation ceremony and the relation of the witnesses to the denouncer as well as the denounced. The denouncer and the denounced alone do not constitute a degradation ceremony (unless viewed from a psychological viewpoint). Degradation ceremonies occur only if there are witnesses. To induce shame, the denouncer must convince a group of witnesses to view the event in a special way. "The paradigm of moral indignation," Garfinkel says, "is 'public' denunciation. We publicly deliver the curse: 'I call upon all men to bear witness that he is not as he appears but is otherwise and in essence of a lower species'" (1956, 421).

In a systematic manner, Garfinkel accounts for the method that must be followed. First, the denouncer needs to demonstrate to witnesses that he and they share fundamental values. Second, the denouncer needs to demonstrate that the denounced does not share these values. Moreover, the denouncer needs to show that the reason the denounced does not share these values is based on choice rather than conditions. While the denounced may seem to hold the shared values of the community, the denouncer must show that the denounced does not and never really did. "The work of the denunciation," Garfinkel asserts, "effects the recasting of the objective character of the perceived other: The other person becomes in the eyes of his condemners literally a different and *new* person. It is not that the new attributes are added to the old 'nucleus.' He is not changed, he is reconstituted" (1956, 421).

The denouncer must show as well that he or she is a legitimate and objective spokesperson for those values that the denouncer and witnesses share and from which the denouncer claims that the denounced is estranged. If the degradation ceremony is to be successful, the denouncer must show that the denounced chose to be estranged from the values that the denouncer and witnesses share, not because of unfavorable conditions or unfortunate circumstances, but because of the choice of the denounced. The denouncer must clearly expose the denounced's motive. The denouncer must show that the denounced's motive is the only thing that is relevant to his or her behavior. No circumstances or loopholes can be found. Degradation ceremonies, Garfinkel insists, are never successful unless all these criteria are met. If the denouncer fails to meet any, the degradation ceremony misses its mark.

It is important to address the reasons why the gunman's attempted degradation ceremony fails. The gunman fails in his attempt to debase you because he cannot be a legitimate spokesperson for the values he claims to share with his witnesses when he flagrantly violates these values. This event is the gunman's idea, and you are the object of the gunman's projection. Your selection is arbitrary; it has no relation to you as a particular person. Your motive—your intention as a social actor—is, from the viewpoint of the gunman, irrelevant. The gunman cannot denounce you if the reason for the conduct for which you are being denounced is entirely coerced by him. This factor alone short-circuits the gunman's attempted degradation ceremony.

From the perverse viewpoint of the gunman, however, his activity is partially successful. What conditions exist that allow him to think this way? During the war in Bosnia, the world watched through the news media. The world played the role of witness. UN peacekeepers in particular played this role. The gazing world thus became a sustaining component of the system that perpetuated ethnic cleansing. Nationalist Serbs played the role of denouncers; the others, whether Kosovar Albanians, Croats, Bosnian Muslims, or Serbian opposition, were the ones denounced; and the gazing world was the witness to the ritual. As long as nationalist Serbs sustained this triadic structure and as long as witnesses allowed nationalist Serbs to sustain it, ethnic cleansing persisted. By insisting on their "simulated" privilege to assume the role of denouncer, nationalist Serbs blocked those whom they degraded from denouncing them for war crimes and crimes against humanity. The way to avoid being denounced was to pervert the very resource required for denunciation. To avoid becoming the subject of a renunciation, nationalist Serbs co-opted an unqualified privilege to engage in renunciation.

For the watching world, the role of witness to the ritual of ethnic cleansing becomes problematic. Serving as witness to evil is untenable. The role creates dissonance. With whom do the witnesses identify: the denouncers, the Serbian nationalists who confess a Christian faith as Orthodox Serbs, or the denounced, the Bosnian Muslims who follow the Islamic faith? Nationalist Serbs exploited this difference, which gave them status in the Western press and a rhetorical advantage with viewers who were predominantly Christian.

As time passed and ethnic cleansing persisted, it became more and more unclear who were the objects of the degradation ceremony called ethnic cleansing. It was no accident that during their activity ethnic cleansers would select the weakest individuals from their victims to be present. Consider this example.

> One of the Serb soldiers came into the room and turned to me and started to beat me, especially on my head and spine, and I fainted. Two days later, I had my first epileptic seizure. When the Serbs from the camp heard about this, they took me to watch them torture others. They were sure I was going to die. I was very weak; my weight was down to 36 kilos, and I could only walk with difficulty. One night, two soldiers came in and took me to an area where they hung people. I saw one man hung through his back on the hook of the lift for a lorry. He was still alive and screaming. And yet the Serbs went on beating him. On the floor was another man whose skin was split; he was dead. . . . Throughout the night

they ordered me to watch the torture, while they laughed. When I returned to the room, I had another epileptic seizure. (Mešinović 1993, 6)

Ethnic cleansers designated the role of witness because it was an essential component of their activity. They then released these individuals, assuming they would be too degraded to tell the world what happened and what they observed.

The world did not volunteer for the role of the witness. Indeed, whenever the world tried to disassociate itself from this relationship, ethnic cleansers sensationalized their brutality to such a degree that it was impossible for the rest of the world to remove itself. The more the world resisted being implicated in the process of ethnic cleansing, the more nationalist Serbs manipulated the world into their project. Eventually, the world became not only the witness, but also the object of this degradation ceremony.

The gunman, for instance, was not trying to shame you; he was trying to shame your relation to the world. He was trying to destroy the fact that the world and you share fundamental values—values such as fatherhood, compassion, and love—from which the gunman himself was estranged. The gunman, not you, was the pariah. The more estranged the gunman was from the world, the more he wanted to estrange you from the world and the world from itself.

Only in this way can the gunman presume to be a legitimate spokesperson for the world. As long as the world stands for nothing, the gunman becomes its spokesperson. The gunman comes to represent the world. If the postmodern integrity of the world is to stand for nothing, the gunman presumes to speak for this world and its relation to you, that is, this world's nonrelation to you as well as to itself. To "misapply" a citation from Garfinkel, "The denouncer must make the dignity of the supra-personal values of the tribe salient and accessible to view, and his denunciation must be delivered in their name" (1956, 423). In a nihilistically guided lifeworld, the gunman is able to be just such a denouncer.

Soon you, the father, begin to see that the world, more than you, is being denounced. Your role at this point changes. You become not the one being denounced, but the witness to the denunciation of the world. That is, you become the witness to the denunciation of the witness to your denunciation. You, the father, pity the world. You become, as it were, the witness to evil's defilement of humanity. When the world gazed upon Bosnia, it saw itself as the object of evil's denunciation; the world became riveted to the conduct of ethnic cleansing. Bosnia became ground zero because in Bosnia the world witnessed its own denunciation.

As noted, the logic, the latent function that guided ethnic cleansing, was to bind the wavering and ambivalent Bosnian Serbs together within a band of collective guilt. As it became more and more impossible for Bosnian Serbs to disassociate themselves from this evil (although many did and still do), the logic consumed itself. New fuel was needed. The more the world watched, the more the world itself became included in the band of collective guilt originally meant first to bind together the Serbian people.

Thus, what fueled the ego of the gunman was his ability to bully the conscience of the world, that is, his ability to submit the world's conscience to his will. What fueled the ego of the gunman was his ability to force the world to repress its conscience, its superego, to the same degree and in the same manner that the gunman repressed his own. As ethnic cleansing persisted, the ways in which the gunman and the world were alike became more and more important, and the ways in which the gunman and the father were not alike became less and less important.

The goal of evil is to destroy humanity, what Karl Marx refers to as the human species-being. Evil achieves its purpose by claiming not just that one person is a non–human being, but that the notion of human being in itself is nonexistent. Evil relativizes the human species-being, mocks its innate significance. When evil is successful, humanity loses its capacity to be itself; humanity is no longer capable of making its members or itself whole. The vitality of humanity is concealed.

At such points, humanity's absence becomes poignantly conspicuous, which provokes its imminent return. Humanity is resilient in ways that cannot be grasped empirically or predicted scientifically. The disassociation that evil seeks is thus never fully realized because of the nonempirical character of humanity itself. The knowledge of a person that one gains from the degradation ceremony is merely situational; it lacks a relation to what is essential to the person per se. Human beings are created beings. Martin Buber proclaims this point poignantly when he says, "And in all the seriousness of truth, hear this: without *It* man cannot live. But he who lives with *It* alone is not a man" (1987, 34).

5. Rape as Evil

A while back a European Commission of Inquiry headed by Dame Anne Warburton made a study in the former Yugoslavia and reported that 20,000 women had been raped. *New York Times* correspondent John Burns puts the number at 50,000. Michigan law professor Catharine A. MacKinnon, who is representing Bosnian victims pro bono, puts the total at "more than 50,000" women and girls raped, and another 100,000 women and children killed.

—Grace Halsell

The rapes that occurred in Bosnia during the war were assaults on individuals' bodies and selves. The purpose was not just to harm a woman or young girl's body, although this was one purpose. The purpose was also to destroy a person's sense of self as a free and self-conscious person. The damage that rape does to the self, while sometimes invisible, takes longer to heal than the damage done to the body, although the harm to the body and the harm to the self are both acts of injustice.

In Bosnia, rape had an even more wretched significance. The purpose was to destroy the woman's relation to her family and community, in part by provoking her family and community to reject her. The rapes sought to destroy the person's sense of identity and connectedness to

---

An earlier version of this chapter appeared in *Sociologija nakon Bosne* and *Sociology after Bosnia and Kosovo: Recovering Justice*.

those whom she loved and who loved her. Rape was done knowing that it could lead to the person being rejected by her parents, her husband, and even her children. In other words, rape was an attempt to destroy the person's interconnectedness with her family. Rape was an attempt to turn a person into a nonhuman, an animal, by taking from a person what distinguishes the person's humanity.

What is the essence of humanity? Karl Marx writes, "The animal is immediately identical with its life activity. It does not distinguish itself from itself. It is *its life-activity*. [Human beings] make their life activity itself the object of [their] will and [their] consciousness. [Human beings] have conscious life activity. . . . Conscious life-activity directly distinguishes [humans] from animal life-activity" (2004, 34). Rape is a vicious assault against the human species-being.

Consider the following testimonies. The painfulness of the testimonies is based on both the physical harm done to the person and the damage to the person's sense of interdependency that is the social life of the person.

> A doctor from my same town was prisoner here. One day the Serbian guards called for this doctor. They wanted him to sew up a ten-year-old girl they had raped. She was torn apart. Seeing the mutilated child, the doctor forgot he was a prisoner, and that he was in a concentration camp. He cursed the Serbs, telling them, "You are not human!" According to Issa, the guards left the child bleeding on the table and assaulted the doctor. Issa said that when she again saw the doctor, "He was barely alive." (Halsell 1993)

The doctor's curse is a reminder to the rapists of their species-being, and that the rapists could not tolerate. The rapists, to achieve their evil purpose, sever their own relation to their human species-being; they forget their mothers, their sisters, their wives, their daughters, and their granddaughters. They lose their consciousness, often through drinking. After raping a woman, they, though, will not forget her, and they will remember her, if only unconsciously, whenever they are intimate with another woman.

Consider another testimony:

> Refugees from Srebrenica thought the worst was over when they reached a UN base at Potočari, two miles north of the fallen safe haven. But it was there, despite the presence of Dutch peace keepers, that Ms. Turković says Bosnian Serbs chose a young victim

from among the sleeping refugees. "Two took her legs and raised them up in the air, while the third began raping her," Ms. Turković said. "Four of them were taking turns on her. People were silent, no one moved. She was screaming and yelling and begging them to stop. They put a rag into her mouth and then we were just hearing silent sobs coming from her closed lips. "When they finished, the woman was left there," she said. (Vukić 1995)

The assault on this young woman is unconscionable and unthinkable. It is a direct assault against not only her body and her self, but also her family and her community. It is an assault that attempts to destroy the bonds of care that hold the young woman and her community together. The place and the timing of the rape are utterly obscene.

Bosnian soldiers created rape camps as described in the following testimony.

We had to cook for them, and serve them, naked. They raped and slaughtered some girls right in front of us. Those who resisted had their breasts cut. One night Željka's brother helped twelve of us escape. . . . Sometimes I think I will go crazy. Every night in my dreams I see the face of Stojan, the camp guard. He was the most ruthless among them. He even raped ten-year-old girls, as a "delicacy." Most of those girls didn't survive. They murdered many girls, slaughtered them like cattle. I want to forget everything. I cannot live with these memories. I will go insane. (Mirsada 1997)

In such rape camps, the species-being of the person is assaulted and denied, if not seemingly destroyed. The rape camp is designed to force the person to give up her species-being because retaining it becomes itself a source of horror and pain. Witnessing these brutalities against others and oneself is venomous to the person's species-being. Rape is a war crime because it is an attempt to destroy a community and sever the bonds of interdependency based on care and trust. Such bonds are what hold communities and families together. The premeditated and methodic use of rape to attack and destroy the foundation of community is evil.

A profound documentary on this difficult subject is *Calling the Ghosts*, distributed by Women Make Movies. It is exceptional because it shows that the species-being of the people apprehended and abused was not destroyed. The species-being of the people survived beyond the unspeakable experiences for those who survived and beyond the point of death for those who perished. Witnessing the moments of care and self-consciousness on the part of the people who lived through a hellish experience in Omarska is a testimony to the human spirit. People remembered their universality based on their connectedness to others and the world. This universality exemplified their freedom even during their most unfree moments. The willingness of the people who suffered so much to share their compelling self-consciousness is something that the world needs to listen to and be grateful for. The people who suffered in Bosnia bear witness to the indestructible and immortal character of the human species-being. The world will be impoverished if it does not accept this gift and understand its lesson. Here is one such gift from Hasiba Harambašić, as recorded in *Calling the Ghosts*.

> You see a friend who has several cuts on his throat. His collar bone is broken and his arm is hanging limp. He is all beaten up, in bruises—I get chills when I think of him and how he looked—bloody, torn, full of lice, a mess. Everyone had dysentery, so everyone stunk. It was suffocating. But that man, truly a gentleman, at that moment when he passes us by, he makes sure that his shirt collar is closed. He holds it with his hand so we don't see his wounds, so we are less afraid. Can you imagine what that looks like? Scenes like that were going on twenty-four hours a day.

6. Evil's Agency

For every one who does evil hates the light, and does not come to the light, lest his deeds should be exposed.

—John 3:20

What is the relation between an intellectual's work and an intellectual's life? Is it fair to measure one against the other? Does the knowledge of how an intellectual debased his or her life contribute to a critical understanding of an intellectual's work? Shall we keep the two separate? Shall we fail to consider the two together?

Mihailo Marković is a world-renowned Yugoslav philosopher recognized for his writing on humanism, social democracy, and human rights. He was a leading member of the editorial board of *Praxis* and director of the famous Korčula Summer School. His biography as a military officer in Tito's partisan army made him a charismatic figure among intellectuals in North America and Europe. In 1975, the Serbian Parliament brought charges of political deviance against Marković and seven other academicians; they were removed from their university positions on charges of corrupting the youth. The group became known as the Belgrade 8; protests from American professors such as Noam Chomsky, Daniel Bell, and Stanley Hoffman did not change the Yugoslav government's decision against the group. *Praxis* was banned (Secor 1999).

An earlier version of this chapter was published as "Intellektualna Izdaja i Bosanskohercegovačka Muka" in *Odjek*.

In Marković's well-known book *From Affluence to Praxis: Philosophy and Social Criticism*, Erich Fromm (1974, ix) writes in the "Foreword":

This work . . . is not facile, and "food" for those who like simplified arguments. It is thorough and honest, and I hope that it will interest many people who are fed up with "revolutionary" phrasemaking presented as brilliant "reinterpretations" of Marx.

First, what is *praxis*? It is the strong reformulation of what Karl Marx means by the life-activity of the human species-being. It is the contrasting, positive principle to human alienation. In Marx's writing, alienation is where human beings are disconnected from their conscious life-activity; *praxis* is where they are connected with it. *Praxis* is the non-metaphysical product of human work and the resource for meaningful social relations.

Marković published widely on *praxis*. He helped develop an independent, critical, humanistic version of Marxism on behalf of social democracy. Indeed, there are three scholarly books that focus specifically on Marković's work; these are Gerson S. Sher's (1977) *Praxis: Marxist Criticism and Dissent in Socialist Yugoslavia,* David A. Crocker's (1983) *Praxis and Democratic Socialism: The Critical Social Theory of Marković and Stojanović,* and Oskar Gruenwald's (1983) *The Yugoslav Search for Man: Marxist Humanism in Contemporary Yugoslavia.*

Marković also held numerous visiting academic positions in the United States. In 1961–62, he received a Ford Foundation Grant at the University of California. In 1967–68, he lectured at American universities; he was a visiting professor at the University of Michigan (1969–70) and at the University of Pennsylvania (1972–73 and 1975–76). Marković was also a visiting professor at Haverford College, where Richard J. Bernstein helped secure him this academic post.

What is now intellectually vexatious and morally disheartening is that Marković became a major supporter of Slobodan Milošević. He was a key ideologue in Milošević's political party responsible for planning, initiating, and carrying out war crimes and crimes against humanity in Bosnia-Herzegovina. In her book, *The Destruction of Yugoslavia: Tracking the Break-up 1980–92,* Branka Magaš introduces the pivotal role that Marković played.

I remember the feeling of fear provoked by seeing the signatures of Mihailo Marković . . . on this petition, fear produced by my realization that such a rallying to nationalism of Serbia's progressive intelligentsia meant that civil war was now in the cards. (1993, 4)

Marković became not a passive spectator, but a significant player on behalf of Milošević's rise to power. He helped navigate the Serbian people into the jaws of racist nationalism. He steered the wheel at the helm.

This unexpected, indeed astonishing, alignment of *Praxis* editors with nationalism has aroused considerable dismay among their friends and sympathizers, for it delineates a complete break with the political and philosophical tradition represented by the journal. (Magaš 1993, 52)

The role that Marković played on behalf of Milošević's Belgrade regime must not be understated; he is tantamount to an intellectual war criminal.

This dramatic betrayal of the principles of humanistic philosophy and critical theory did not go utterly unnoticed. Joseph H. Carens (1993) published an anthology titled *Democracy and Possessive Individualism: The Intellectual Legacy of C. B. Macpherson*, to which Marković had contributed an essay. In light of Marković's political activities in former-Yugoslavia, Carens wrestled with the decision of whether to include Marković's essay in the anthology. In a letter to *The Times Literary Supplement* titled "Scholarship and Ethnic Cleansing," Carens wrote this statement.

I feel obliged not to pass over in silence the apparent contradiction between the theory that one of the contributors—Mihailo Marković—has espoused here, and the practice he has followed as a political figure in Serbia today. . . . Marković argued long ago that socialism must respect democracy and human rights. He was penalized severely for taking this stand in Yugoslavia. . . . How are we to reconcile these admirable thoughts and these principled commitments with the fact that Mihailo Marković served from 1990 until November of 1992 as the Vice-President of the Serbian Socialist Party? This is the governing party in Serbia, the party whose president is Slobodan Milošević, the political leader of Serbia. Milošević's regime has promoted precisely the sort of extreme and vicious nationalism that has expressed itself through violence and military aggression. (1993, 15)

Carens is open and forthright. Interestingly, in the same issue of *The Times Literary Supplement*, Marković published a rebuttal:

> The entire world was shocked by dreadful pictures of people killed by explosions while they were waiting for bread in Vase Miskina Street in Sarajevo in late May 1992. The crime was attributed to Serbs. This was the immediate reason for the UN Security Council introducing sanctions against Yugoslavia on May 31, 1992. The truth about the event was revealed with considerable delay, owing to the report of the Canadian General MacKenzie who, at that moment, was the commander of the UN peace forces in Sarajevo. And the truth is that it was Bosnian Muslims who set the mines that killed all those innocent people, including a number of Muslims. They did it deliberately in order to put the blame on Serbs and have them satanized in front of the entire world. A little later came the story about detention camps in which Serbs were allegedly keeping dozens of thousands of Bosnian Muslim civilians, women and children. Dozens of delegations, journalists, and human rights defenders tried to substantiate these charges—without any success. There are no such camps, nothing except a few centres for prisoners of war, which are in much better shape than those camps in which Muslims and Croats detain Serbs. The next story, to which Joe Carens refers in the beginning of his note, was the one describing the systematic raping of Muslim women by Bosnian Serbs. . . . No one mentions any numbers any more. The entire story was based on hearsay. . . . What I firmly deny is that there was any deliberate systematic activity of this kind. (1993, 16)

It is difficult to imagine how Marković could write such a piece for *The Times Literary Supplement*. The crime that took place on Vise Miskina Street in late May 1992 was attributed to the Serb forces surrounding Sarajevo. While Canadian General MacKenzie was the commander of the UN peace forces in Bosnia, he colluded with nationalist Serb forces. Since the war, MacKenzie has been a public speaker on behalf of the nationalist Serb party line in former-Yugoslavia. Detention camps—in which nationalist Serbs were keeping hundreds of thousands of civilians—have been carefully and fully documented; the systematic raping of Muslim women by Bosnian Serbs has been carefully and fully documented. With his rebuttal in *The Times Literary Supplement*, Marković used his academic reputation to protect war criminals and allow them to continue to commit crimes against humanity with impunity. He engaged in propaganda to conceal the truth about the war crimes and crimes against humanity occurring in Bosnia.

Marković was an accomplice of evil. He helped concoct the toxic cynicism that triggered and enflamed Serbian nationalism. Besides the earlier comment in *The Times Literary Supplement*, Marković made comparable propagandistic comments in other prestigious publications. In an article in the *New York Times* titled, "A Sort of 'Super Serb' Defends Serbian Policy," Marković is cited as defending the war aims of Belgrade's aggression against Bosnia.

> I don't understand why there is so much outside opposition to cantonization. It would end the fighting in 24 hours. The alternative is the creation of a Muslim state in the heart of Europe. . . . But we find this very disturbing . . . and we don't like the idea that Turkey, which invaded our land and ruled us for 400 years, would consider this territory as part of the Muslim world. (Kinzer 1992, 5)

Bosniaks (Bosnian Muslims) are not Turkish; they are Southern Slavs like Bosnian Croats and Bosnian Serbs. From the eleventh to the fourteenth century, before falling to the Ottoman invasion, Bosnia had enjoyed its own medieval state. Then, for four hundred years under Ottoman rule, Bosnia was a separate and legally defined provincial entity. From 1878 to 1918, under Austro-Hungarian rule, Bosnia-Herzegovina remained a legally defined and undivided provincial entity. Under Austro-Hungarian rule, Bosnia came to be called Bosnia-Herzegovina. Within the federal republic of Yugoslavia from 1945–91, Bosnia-Herzegovina was a republic within the federation of Yugoslavia just like Slovenia, Macedonia, Croatia, Montenegro, and Serbia. Marković's comment in the *New York Times* fogs the historical and political reality of the situation. His comment mimes the vulgarity of Serbian nationalism, a racist ideology that fueled sociocide.

Consider also Marković's interview for *The Chronicle of Higher Education* in the article titled, "Serbia's Academic Apologists."

> A handsome man of 70 who speaks fluent English and is thoroughly familiar with Western societies, he has tried to convince

skeptical intellectuals in the West that Serbs were not the instigators of the Bosnian war but were, instead, its victims.

He likens Mr. Milošević to Abraham Lincoln. "Lincoln is a great man even though he presided during the war in which 600,000 persons died," he says. The destruction of Sarajevo and other cities is to be expected in a civil war, he adds. "General Sherman not only occupied Atlanta, but burned it to the ground, and then did the same up and down the coast."

"The United States was founded on the basis of ethnic cleansing. It was a terrible thing—the taking of Indian lands—but it was ethnic cleansing. Germany engaged in the ethnic cleansing of Slavs. History does not follow the same rhythm everywhere." Here in the territories of the former Yugoslavia, he says, "phenomena are occurring that took place in the rest of Europe back in the 19th century." (Doder 1993, 17)

With a vulgar sense of historicism, Marković justifies urbicide and genocide. From the viewpoint of realpolitik, he attempts to explain the amoral political significance of ethnic cleansing to the global academy. Marković faithfully served Milošević, the demagogue who was an incarnation of every principle Marković resisted and critically analyzed as a humanist and critical theorist.

How could Marković join with Milošević? Consider some of the following quotations from Marković's writing that Oskar Gruenwald cites, "Some Marxists (although by no means only Marxists) have been behaving as though they accepted 'the end-justifies-the-means' principle. . . . [Marxist humanism] rejects both this principle and the practice of permanent subordination of morals (and science, and law, and art) to politics. . . . There are certain elements (truths, values) of lasting human significance that are not relative to place and time" (1983, 4–5). Gruenwald then gives his own commentary on the importance of Marković's work:

> Marković, like Djilas, Mihajlov, and others before him, minces no words in defining the essential prerequisites for a genuinely self-governing, democratic as well as socialist society:
>
> What is needed is the existence of a strong and free public opinion, and that means: Intensive political life without authoritarian subordination and manipulation, unhindered circulation of ideas, freedom of public criticism, and independent means of mass communication.
>
> (1983, 11–12)

How could Marković turn against the integrity of his theoretical work in such a transgressive way? Did Marković forget himself? Is it fair now to measure Marković's intellectual work against his political life? Does the knowledge of how Marković acted on behalf of Serbian nationalism and its genocidal aggression against his fellow citizens and former colleagues initiate a critical understanding of Marković's writing? Is there anything in Marković's work that suggests such a turn of events? Do the numerous scholars in Europe and North America who learned from Marković in the past have an obligation to critically revisit this resource (McBride 2001)?

At this point, it could be said that the political actions of Marković entrap critical theory. Critical theory claims to be able to answer the question of what it means to speak with moral authority in the social realm; the contrast between Marković's theorizing and political actions belies this claim. Moreover, the notable silence of the community of critical theorists on this issue is difficult to fathom. Why have Marković's former colleagues and professional friends not publicly objected to Marković's propaganda supporting evil?

The purpose of Milošević's campaign against Bosnia was to murder a vibrant culture that enjoyed a diverse and multiconfessional heritage for centuries (Banac 1993, Bringa 2002, Donia and Fine 1994, Mahmutčehajić 2000, Malcolm 1994); the intent was to destroy a functional community that authentically exemplified multiculturalism. On the one hand, Marković's work in critical theory exemplifies a biophilic attitude toward humanity and society; on the other hand, his conduct as a political and intellectual leader of Serbian nationalism exemplifies a necrophilic attitude toward different communities and the human beings within them.

Consider the two tacks that could be taken: one tack argues that Marković betrayed his earlier principles as a humanist Marxist, the principles that won him respect and admiration from many scholars in Europe and North America. That is, Marković forgot the ideas of moral integrity articulated in his earlier theorizing. If this tack is taken, the critique of Marković's recent conduct becomes a tacit endorsement of his past work. Marković simply becomes an apostate of his former commitment to critical theory.

Consider, however, the second tack: it argues that there is something in Marković's writing that allows us to anticipate his political actions. That is, there is something in Marković's writing that allows us not to be surprised by his ignoble conduct supporting and planning Milošević's genocidal campaign of terror throughout former-Yugoslavia. If, indeed, there is something there in Marković's writing, what is it? And if there is something there, why did colleagues not catch it? Is it something that is perhaps also present in their work?

Marković's betrayal challenges critical theory. Critical theorists, especially those who knew Marković personally, need to address this challenge publicly, not privately. What did intellectuals miss in the sixties, seventies, and eighties when they passionately promoted Marković's career and his writing in critical theory? What did they fail to recognize as problematic in not only Marković's work, but also their own?

What is *praxis*? Again, *praxis* is the strong reformulation of what Karl Marx means by the life-activity of the human species-being. In Marx's writing, *praxis* is the positive concept contrasting human alienation. *Praxis* gives dialectical weight to Marx's analysis of capitalism. It is the nonmetaphysical foundation for the life-activity of the human species, that is, work; it is the resource for meaningful relations; it is the collective and shared product of a nonalienated community of human beings. While alienation is where human beings remain unconnected to their life-activity, *praxis* is the principle through which they remain connected.

What then is Marković's particular understanding of *praxis*? Why was Marković's particular understanding so widely acclaimed? David Crocker's exegetical discussion of Marković's writing is helpful.

> Marković believes that Maslow has identified and operationally defined these best human beings' objective traits, such as openness to experience, objectivity, spontaneity, and ability to love, and their corresponding subjective attitudes, such as zest, self-confidence in handling stress, and serenity. Moreover, these operational definitions have been accomplished, claims Marković, without derivation from a higher-order of normative principle. (1977, 29)

Empirically, for Marković, indicators of *praxis* would be openness to experience, objectivity, spontaneity, and the ability to love. Psychologically, indicators would be zest, self-confidence in handling stress, and serenity. Marković argues that such indicators can be reliably established without derivation from a higher-order of normative principle.

This epistemology is repeated in other contexts. Marković formulates six dispositions of *praxis*: (1) intentionality, (2) freedom as self-determination, (3) creativity, (4) sociality, (5) rationality, and (6) individual self-realization. Crocker explains the relation and interdependency of these six dispositions.

> Instead of being a more fundamental principle from which the six dispositions are deduced, justified, or explained, the concept of *praxis* is defined in terms of and is a verbal shorthand for action that realizes the six dispositions. Yet this pluralism of normative principles is of a special kind for an action cannot be *praxis* unless *all* six are realized together, and Marković intends to define the six principles in such a way that conflict among them is conceptually impossible. (1977, 11)

The relation among the six optimal dispositions of *praxis* is pluralistic. Metaphysics is absent. There is no transcendental principle here. The six optimal dispositions cannot be derived from a higher order of normative principle.

Marković's account of *praxis* is strikingly analogous to the ancient sophist's account of virtue. The analogy is useful for framing Marković's particular understanding of *praxis*. In *Protagoras*, Socrates asks Protagoras what is the relation between virtue as a whole and the individual virtues like courage, piety, beauty, wisdom, temperance, and justice. Protagoras answers that virtue is one and the qualities Socrates asks about are parts of it (Plato 1975, 61). Marković would likewise say that the concept of *praxis* is one and the six optimal dispositions are parts.

What is interesting is not whether the metaphysical list of ancient virtues matches the empirical list of modern virtues; what is interesting is the way in which Protagoras and Marković's sense of the relation between the different elements of their respective lists is comparable. In contrast to Protagoras, Marković would say that *praxis* is not one but many parts. That is, *praxis* is only its parts. *Praxis* is simply a sum of parts; it is not a whole, a unity. *Praxis* is not really even a sum of its parts because there is no "it" which would gather together the parts as something of which they are a part. *Praxis* instead is simply a nominal label for the sum of the parts that constitute it.

Socrates then asks Protagoras how the different virtues—justice, temperance, beauty, piety, wisdom, courage—are part of virtue, the whole. Are they parts of the whole like parts of a face—mouth, nose, eyes, and ears—with different characteristics and functions, or like parts of a piece of gold, which do not differ from one another or from the whole except in size (Plato 1975, 61)? In the first case, a part, for example, justice, has a distinct function and does not resemble the other parts. For instance, justice is distinct from temperance in the same way that the eye is distinct from the ear. Each part of the face has a distinct function; each part is independent of the whole.

For a modern version of this relation, consider Émile Durkheim's (1964) notion of organic solidarity to explain the nature of social order in light of modern civilization and the industrial revolution. Given the division of labor, members of society are unique, each with a specialized and irreplaceable occupation. However, as Durkheim stresses in *The Division of Labor in Society*, members remain socially connected like the parts of the face are connected to one another even though members' occupations and lives are unique and specialized. For Durkheim, the challenge for modern sociology is to identify the basis of this solidarity.

Consider now the second case, when the different virtues—justice, temperance, beauty, piety, wisdom, courage—are like pieces of gold and the different virtues are more alike than they are different. They are different only in terms of weight and size like pieces of gold.

For the sociological example of this relation, consider Durkheim's notion of mechanical solidarity. In contrast to organic solidarity, members of society have solidarity because of their commonness rather than their uniqueness. One member is essentially interchangeable with another. To know one member is thus to know the whole. An Amish community would be a contemporary example of mechanical solidarity.

To explain the relation between virtue as a whole and its parts, Protagoras does not consider this second case. As a harbinger of modern thought, Protagoras answers that the different virtues are parts in the first way, like parts of a face. Justice and temperance are unlike each other in the same way that the eye and the ear are unlike each other (Plato 1975, 61).

Marković's reasoning is analogous to that of Protagoras. For Marković, the relation between the six optimal dispositions of *praxis*—intentionality, freedom as self-determination, creativity, sociality, rationality, and individual self-realization—is like the relation of the parts of the face. There is not a whole that collects these distinct dispositions. The six optimal dispositions are not like pieces of gold that differ from each other and the whole in terms of size.

Later in the dialogue, Socrates asks Protagoras the following question: If justice and holiness, two different virtues, fail to resemble each other and fail as well to resemble the whole, could one then be just, truly just, without being holy or holy, truly holy, without being just? At this point, Protagoras balks and begrudgingly begins to rethink his answer. A refutation occurs, and the refutation is based on Protagoras's recognition of the limit of his argument. It is unintelligent to argue that one could be just while being unholy or that one could be holy while being unjust (Plato 1975, 63–64).

Would Marković balk and begrudgingly begin to rethink his position? Marković says that the distinct parts of *praxis* coincide without conceptual conflict. The distinct parts coincide without conceptual conflict, however, only insofar as there is no concept within which they coincide. There is nothing inherent or intrinsically significant to *praxis* in and of itself. Conceptual conflict between the parts is impossible in that there is no whole within which conflict occurs. The whole is randomness, at best. In Marković's reasoning, one's practice can exemplify intentionality but not creativity, sociality but not rationality, individual self-realization but not freedom as self-realization.

What would these combinations look like? What is *praxis* that is intentionality but not freedom as self-determination? What is *praxis* that is creativity but not individual self-realization? The combinations are jarring in their irrationality. They are jarring in the same manner that the combination of being just but unholy or holy but unjust are jarring. Unless the six optimal dispositions that constitute Marković's concept of *praxis* are seen as coinciding within a whole, "a higher order of normative principle," it is difficult to see how Marković's notion of what good practice is is anything except chaos. Marković's understanding of *praxis* is nihilistic. Marković's theorizing within the tradition of critical theory foreshadows, indeed predicts, his bad faith with which he cynically supported and promoted evil in Bosnia.

Within the tradition of social science, critical theory is the guardian of dialectical reasoning and defender of its transcendental principles for the enlightened understanding of human beings within society. Today, Marković is a problem for critical theory. A significant body of scholarly literature focuses on Martin Heidegger's membership in the Nazi

Party and the relation between Heidegger's philosophy and his political actions. The central polemic in this scholarly literature is stated by Richard Wolin: "The more one learns about Heidegger's relations with National Socialism, the more one is ineluctably driven to conclude that the philosopher himself perceived his Nazi involvements not as a random choice of action, but as a *logical outgrowth of his philosophical doctrines*" (1993, 273). It is time to raise the same polemic regarding Marković. Although Marković is not a philosopher of Heidegger's stature, the issues that Marković and Heidegger's biographies raise are comparable. Jacques Derrida makes the argument that it is the surplus of metaphysical thinking in Heidegger's work that accounts for Heidegger's ignoble conduct (Wolin 1993, 288). The argument here is the opposite: it is the deficiency of metaphysical thinking in Marković's work that explains his ignoble promotion of genocide in Bosnia. Consider the following passage from "Humanism and Dialectic," an early essay by Marković: "A humanist axiology is a theory of concrete, historically given and variable values—not of certain absolute, transcendental ideals or norms" (Marković 1966, 85).

Marković has had extremely supportive colleagues in North America, for instance, Richard J. Bernstein, Seyla Benhabib, and William J. McBride. These friends would do well to carefully listen to the resistance that Marković receives from his own colleagues in Belgrade. To give one example, in *The Politics of Symbol in Serbia: Essays in Political Anthropology*, Ivan Čolović describes the following problem in Marković's account of Serbian nationalism.

> Marković knows "that our heroic choices have regularly entailed enormous sacrifices, suffering, destruction." What is more, he has observed that heroic feats are followed by "great falls." But he mentions these falls only in order to make a contribution to the treatment of that often worn *topos* of the political myth which holds that the enemies of the Serbs achieve in peace what they are unable to in war. "That is when our greatest falls occur," explains Marković, "and then all those who hid in the deepest mouse holes when we were at our height, all those who are overcome by panic-stricken fear whenever it seems to them that we are coming to wake and stir them—then they do with us what they will." In fact, Marković does not make a causal-consequential connection between the "heroic choices" and "great falls," he does not think

that mass loss of life, persecution and suffering could be the reason for the "falls"—they are for him just two historical sequences, which for some reason regularly succeed one another. The Serbian "falls" are in fact unexpected and incomprehensible. (2002, 72)

Marković leaves the relation between the heroic choices of the Serbian people and their great falls unformulated. For Marković, there is no higher order of normative principle with which to explain the relation. Moreover, Marković is oblivious to a third variable—the mass loss of life, persecution, and suffering—that bridges the first two.

7. Evil's Disfigurement of Language

> It is held that man, in distinction from plant and animal, is the living being capable of speech. This statement does not mean only that, along with other faculties, man also possesses the faculty of speech. It means to say that only speech enables man to be the living being he is as man.
>
> —Martin Heidegger

One instrument that promoted evil in Bosnia was the war criminals' mendacious use of language in the media. Documentaries, news reports, and world newspapers featured the verbal utterances of Slobodan Milošević, Ratko Mladić, Željko Ražnjatović (Arkan), and Radovan Karadžić. When speaking with a reporter, Milošević, Mladić, Arkan, and Karadžić were aware of their audience; they anticipated how their audience would perceive them. This awareness influenced what those engaged in evil said and how they said it. The world would think that through these utterances it understood the ineffable events in Bosnia.

Every person engaged in action speaks, and this speaking signifies social membership. Through the mere fact that Milošević, Mladić, Arkan, and Karadžić could be gregarious in the global media, they promoted an image of themselves as members of human society. Despite their crimes against humanity and transgressions against so many communities, they normalized their conduct to themselves and to the world.

An earlier version of this chapter appeared as "O upotrebi dvoličnog diskursa u globalnim medijima od strane počinitelja rathih zločina u Bosni" in *Odjek*.

Their verbal utterances exemplified a pattern that can be identified and critically examined in light of selective writing from Mikhail Bakhtin.

Mikhail Bakhtin lived in Russia from 1895 until 1975. He is a notable linguist and literary theorist whose thought is informed by two dissonant traditions, Marxism and Orthodox Christianity. Bakhtin's analysis of double-voiced discourse in the novels of Fyodor Dostoyevsky is uniquely suitable for examining the rhetoric of war criminals in former-Yugoslavia. The utterances of the guilt-ridden narrator in *Notes from the Underground* and Milošević, Mladić, and others are comparable. The self-consciousness and perverse reflexivity of Dostoyevsky's antihero are also found in the self-presentations of Balkan war criminals in the media.

Let us consider an example. Belgrade Television became an instrument for putting Milošević into power and keeping him there. In *Yugoslavia: Death of a Nation*, Laura Silber and Allan Little state,

> Belgrade Television was firmly in Milošević's grip. It was the ideal tool for stirring up hatred against "the enemies of the Serbian people"—first Kosovo's Albanians, then the Slovenes, the Croats, and finally, the opposition in Serbia itself. After his overwhelming victory in Serbia's first free elections in December, Milošević continued to use the media as his personal propaganda machine, refusing to give the opposition any airtime. To the anti-Communist protestors, Belgrade Television symbolized Milošević's total control over Serbia. (1996, 120)

How did Milošević maintain "total control" over Serbia and, to some degree, the watching world? Belgrade TV would showcase Milošević, and Milošević performed on this stage. What, though, was Milošević's art? The self-consciousness of the antihero in *Notes from the Underground*, as analyzed by Bakhtin, is useful for the explication of the self-presentation of Milošević in the media. Consider this passage from Bakhtin's *Problems of Dostoyevsky's Poetics*.

> In everything he senses above all *someone else's will* predetermining him. It is within the framework of this alien will that he perceives the world order, nature with its mechanical necessity, the social order. His own thought is developed and structured as *the thought of someone personally insulted by the world order*, personally humiliated by its blind necessity. (1984, 236)

Consider now an example from the beginning of Milošević's ascendancy to power.

The crowd roared, screaming for the arrest of the Albanian Party leader. Milošević answered: "I can't hear you, but we will arrest those responsible including those who have used the workers. In the name of the socialist people of Serbia I promise this." Dušan Mitević said it was Milošević at his best. (Silber and Little 1996, 68)

Why does Mitević, chief of Belgrade Television and close confidant of Milošević, say that at this moment Milošević is at his best? What is it about this utterance that is so admirable for Mitević? Milošević hears the crowd screaming for the arrest of Azem Vlasi, the chief of the Communist Party in Kosovo and a Yugoslav Albanian. Milošević says that he cannot hear the crowd well. The crowd, however, knows that Milošević hears it well. Milošević's utterance incites the crowd to rescream what Milošević already hears and what Milošević wants to hear. Milošević acts as if what the crowd wants may be foreign to his mind; he acts as if he is trying unsuccessfully to understand the will of the crowd. The crowd plays the game; it becomes a reflection of Milošević's mind. On the one hand, Milošević appears will-less before the crowd, answering, "I can't hear you." He appears as a blank slate upon which the crowd can implant its sentiments. On the other hand, the will of the crowd seeks only to identify itself with the will of Milošević. The crowd gushes before its demagogue.

Milošević says he will arrest those who deceive the people, who are plotting against Yugoslavia, and who have used the workers. At this very moment, however, it is Milošević who is deceiving the people, plotting against Yugoslavia, and using the workers. The way in which Milošević describes Vlasi (who was an uncooperative party ally in Milošević's effort to oust Ivan Stambolić, the former president of the Republic of Serbia) is, in fact, a description of Milošević. Milošević makes Vlasi his scapegoat. Milošević becomes something other than himself by projecting the charges of which he himself is guilty onto Vlasi. Milošević first transfers his guilt onto Vlasi and then co-opts Vlasi's innocence for himself.

Vlasi is now a simulacrum of what Milošević himself represents. Since Vlasi's simulation of the charges brought against him is unreal,

Milošević's representation of the same charges likewise becomes unreal. Vlasi's simulation of guilt conceals Milošević's representation of guilt. In turn, Vlasi's representation of innocence becomes Milošević's simulation of innocence (Baudrillard 2004, 474).

Bakhtin captures this discursive artfulness and critiques what it is in the following passage:

> In this striving to trample down his own image and his own discourse as they exist in and for the other person, one can hear not only the desire for sober self-definition, but also a desire to annoy the other person; and this forces him to overdo his sobriety, mockingly exaggerating it to the point of cynicism and holy-foolishness. (1984, 232)

In his public utterance, Milošević's lie masks Vlasi's truth. Since the lie and the truth are equally transparent, when juxtaposed, they become equally opaque.

Consider another example. Anthony Borden reports the following media broadcast before Milošević's arrest in Belgrade:

> But soon television footage showed Milošević back at home before a cheering crowd of around 400 die-hard supporters, some of whom were armed. He told Radio B-92 in an extraordinary interview that he was safe, enjoying a cup of coffee. "I'm just drinking coffee with my friends here and I'm just fine, watching all of this like all the citizens of Serbia." (2001)

This utterance is typical of the cynical statements that Milošević made in the media, and it is telltale that Milošević remains "in character" to such a degree before his arrest—as if this technique might somehow save him at the eleventh hour. Milošević identifies with "all the citizens of Serbia," drinking coffee with friends, feeling fine, and Milošević expects them to identify with him, as he does what they themselves do. If Milošević can reassert his solidarity with the people, his impending arrest is derailed. If Milošević's identification is real, his arrest becomes unreal. If the citizens of Serbia see Milošević as one of them, the identification halts his arrest. To understand the character of double-voiced discourse, Bakhtin advises, "Never use for objectifying or finalizing another's consciousness anything that might be inaccessible to that consciousness, that might lie outside its field of vision" (1984, 239), and this discussion of Milošević's utterances follows Bakthin's advice.

Let us turn to a seemingly authorless example of evil's disfigurement of language. On May 27, 1992, a month after the start of the siege of Sarajevo, there was a massacre on Vase Miskina Street. A cameraman for B-H Television, Dževad Čolaković, was working nearby and immediately started to film the wounded, the dead, and their dismembered bodies after the shelling. Vehid Gunić writes, "The viewers have never seen such an appalling sight, even in the most shocking of horror films" (2001, 38). The unedited footage was played on B-H Television, then Eurovision, and then the global media. The viewing of the massacre so shortly after it occurred put the world at the scene of the crime as much as any representation could. The viewing forced the world to witness immediately and directly the criminal actions of Karadžić and his followers.

There was, however, a problem: "It is like truth according to Nietzsche: we no longer believe that the truth is true when all its veils have been removed" (Baudrillard 1995, 77). Gunić then tells about a newscast the same evening by the Serbian and Montenegrin information services.

> That same evening all the Serbian and Montenegrin information services announced that Muslim forces had carried out a massacre in Vase Miskina Street in Sarajevo so as to provoke military intervention in Bosnia and Herzegovina. They adduced as their chief argument for this monstrous lie the fact that our cameraman had been on the spot, which, the Serbian and Montenegrin media claimed, was a sure sign that the Muslims were going to fire on their own people. No greater or more monstrous falsehood has ever been broadcast by any media since the introduction of so-called mass communications. (2001, 39)

Why did the Serbian and Montenegrin information services react so quickly to the B-H Television broadcast? Having this crime witnessed and exposed to the world scared them. The Serbian and Montenegrin information services knew that if this crime were clearly witnessed and fully recognized, the world would intervene, or so they thought. The Serbian and Montenegrin information services were conscious of the world order, they were conscious of their relationship to the world order, and they were conscious of their profound but not absolute separation from it.

On the one hand, the criminals responsible for the massacre at Vase Miskina were barbarians; on the other hand, in an unsuspecting way they were not. The perpetrators of this crime needed to find a way to recast the world's perception of the massacre. If the criminals were absolute barbarians, that is, utterly indifferent to world order, they would not have needed to reframe the event. They would have been indifferent. The criminals, however, were compelled to try to recast the world's perception of the event in order to influence how the world viewed them. The criminals wanted the world to view them as independent of the massacre they caused.

The motivation for military intervention would be to stop injustice and halt the murders of innocents that became sociocide. The Serbian and Montenegrin information services maligned this motivation, which they feared (and unconsciously wanted, given their own inability to stop themselves from inflicting the evil they did). By claiming that "Muslim" forces massacred their own people to make the nationalist Serbian army look bad in the eyes of the world, the Serbian and Montenegrin information services exploited the Western prejudice against Muslims; they tapped the bias in the Western world toward Muslims so as to derail the motivation for intervention.

Notice the transference. The Serbian and Montenegrin information services formulate the "Muslim" forces (the Bosnian government army, in fact, was composed of commanders and soldiers from each ethnic group) as unconscionably manipulative when their utterance is itself unconscionably manipulative. They formulate the other as slaughtering people when it is they, their commanders and soldiers, who are slaughtering people. Their description of the other is a description of themselves. Their utterance functions in a polyphonic way: its manifest function denies their true selves while its latent function bears witness to their true selves. Their utterance sounds both voices, however dissonant, simultaneously.

Denial is achieved through transferring the truth of their action into a false account of the other. As they construct a false account of the other, they simultaneously provide a true account of themselves. They co-opt the other, and the co-optation implicates them in that it covers up as well as reveals what is true about themselves. The victims of the massacre are thus twice victimized. The perpetrators of the crime transfer the stigma of committing the crime to the victims. Not only do the victims suffer the violence, but they also inherit a spurious guilt for inflicting the violence they suffer.

This polyphonic discourse became increasingly powerful as the war progressed, and its function was to keep those responsible for the destruction of Bosnian communities from being brought to justice. These utterances became like another shell, a grenade, to demoralize a community already physically and psychologically traumatized. These utterances camouflaged evil.

Perpetrators of war crimes acted as if they were insulted by the world order and its blind necessity as stated by, for instance, the biblical commandment "Thou shalt not murder." In return, they insulted the world order. The evening newscast of the Serbian and Montenegrin information services showed, in a twisted way, their recognition of the world order. Their recognition, however, surpassed the world order's recognition of itself. It was a hyper-recognition. That is, the world order did not recognize the necessity of its own order; by insulting it, the war criminals humiliated themselves in that they now were the ones reminding the world order of what it failed to witness about itself. A thread of obligation held the war criminals to the world order, a thread for which the war criminals rather than the world order assumed responsibility. This was maddening to the perpetrators of war crimes: it revealed that the war criminals did indeed know what they were not supposed to know. It revealed that they knew even better than the world order what the world order was itself supposed to know. This only incensed the war criminals to increase their efforts to mock the world order that acted ignorant of its own character. Although expected and hoped for in March 1992 after the tragedy on Vase Miskina Street, intervention was not forthcoming massacre after massacre. Not only victims, but also victimizers were astonished at the lack of meaningful intercession from the international community to the occurrence of sociocide in Europe.

The terror of the shell in Vase Miskina was matched by the terror of the chatter in the Serbian and Montenegrin news. The massacre represented senseless, unbounded violence; the broadcast was unbounded by truth and integrity. The utterance became a parody of the slaughter, a parody that echoed "the noiseless noise" of the shell. The utterance's purpose was to conceal an understanding of the shell's nihilism, despite the clear witnessing of the slaughter on the global media.

Pragmatically, everyone understood why the international community did not intervene—conditions and politics were exceedingly complex. Morally, nobody understood why the international community did not intervene. Both moral imperatives and international law demanded intervention. The war criminals recognized that they had no other choice but to repeat and intensify their crimes until the world order was forced to come to terms with itself and recognize that categorical imperatives ultimately trump utilitarian requirements not only for moral reasons but also for utilitarian reasons. Ironically, evil seeks its own self-destruction through its need to educate, however perversely, the world order about the true character of its own conscience.

In *Anti-Semite and Jew*, Jean-Paul Sartre provides an apt description of what Bakhtin calls holy-foolishness. Although speaking of the language of anti-Semitism in France, Sartre's account can be extended to the language of nationalism in former-Yugoslavia.

> Never believe that anti-Semites are completely unaware of the absurdity of their replies. They know their remarks are frivolous, open to challenge. But they are amusing themselves, for it is their adversary who is obliged to use words responsibly, since he believes in words. The anti-Semites have the *right* to play. They even like to play with discourse for, by giving ridiculous reasons, they discredit the seriousness of their interlocutors. They delight in acting in bad faith, since they seek not to persuade by sound argument but to intimidate and disconcert. If you press them too closely, they will abruptly fall silent, loftily indicating by some phrase that the time for argument is past. It is not that they are afraid of being convinced. They fear only to appear ridiculous or to prejudice by their embarrassment their hope of winning over some third person to their side. (1965, 20)

Sartre's comment advises us in several ways. Never believe, Sartre would tell us, that the perpetrators of war crimes are unaware of the absurdity of their utterances in the media. Never believe that the perpetrators of war crimes do not know that their remarks are frivolous and open to challenge. The perpetrators of war crimes are amusing themselves, and they do not conceal, even from their audience, that they are amusing themselves.

Consider the utterance of Ratko Mladić upon the capture of the UN-declared safe haven, Srebrenica, during the slaughter of thousands of men, as well as the murders and rapes of numerous women and children:

> General Ratko Mladić, commander-in-chief of the Bosnian Serb Army, entered Srebrenica on July 11, 1995, moments behind the first Serb soldiers, accompanied by a television crew. "We present this city to the Serbian people as a gift," Mladić said, speaking to the camera. "Finally, after the rebellion of the Dahis, the time has come to take revenge on the Turks in this region." (Geljten 1997)

"Turk" is a pejorative term that nationalist Serbs use to refer to Bosnian Muslims who, like themselves, are Southern Slavs. What then is this gift that Mladić presents to the Serbian people? If anything, Mladić's attack on Srebrenica and the planned slaughter of thousands curse the Serbian people. Many news reports of this event, however, cite this polyphonic statement from Mladić as if it somehow makes sense of the evil that Mladić commits. Mladić believes he has the right to play with discourse. He shows a sadistic joy in speaking to the world at this particular moment as he enters Srebrenica, and this sadistic joy, at some crude aesthetic level, fascinates the gazing world and fixates it to the speaker's bad faith.

The world is looking for a rationalization for this event that it knows is happening after watching "ethnic cleansing" in Bosnia for years, and Mladić recognizes this need and panders to it by mouthing banal history as an explanation for the violence he is leading. The imperative in Mladić's bad faith is to deny respect for any imperative to which the world order is obliged. By simulating the structure of an ethical imperative, "the time has come," the ethical imperative with which to grasp what Mladić is doing with this utterance is concealed. The purpose of the utterance is to camouflage the evil in Mladić's crimes against humanity. The purpose is to cloak the world's recognition of the occurring crime and thus corrupt the world's will to try to confront and stop the horrendous event before it is completed.

Perpetrators of war crimes use language to discredit the seriousness and responsibility of their interlocutors who would attempt to speak on behalf of justice. The more truthful and responsible their interlocutor, the more empty and ignoble the reply. As Sartre says, "If you press them too closely, they will abruptly fall silent, loftily indicating by some phrase that the time for argument is past" (1965, 20). The more ethically informed the interlocutor, the more debased the response. During the evil inflicted upon Bosnia, this pattern repeated itself many times. The purpose was to intimidate and disconcert; the purpose was identical to that of the shelling. While the shelling has stopped, the verbal assaults have not.

Martin Heidegger writes, "Language speaks. If we let ourselves fall into the abyss denoted by this sentence, we do not go tumbling into emptiness. We fall upward, to a height" (1971, 191). When Mladić speaks, we, however, do go tumbling into emptiness. We fall into the abyss. Even though "language belongs to the closest neighborhood of man's being" (Heidegger 1971, 189), in this case language becomes a stranger to our being. Such is evil's disfigurement of language.

The shells used to commit war crimes in Bosnia-Herzegovina were sometimes measured and studied by military experts. The language used by war criminals needs likewise to be analyzed and critiqued. Bakhtin's work in particular helps with this task. Just as millions of undetonated mines lie in the ground of Bosnia today, hundreds of utterances lie in the memory of Bosnian citizens. Many shells were fired; many utterances spoken. It is imperative to demine these explosives still laying in the fields and homes of Bosnians; it is equally imperative to analyze these utterances. To understand only a few of these may be sufficient to our purpose, which is to explain the nature of evil and critique the perverse model of political discourse that war criminals perpetuate and that so heavily influences our times.

Part 2
Understanding Evil

Paths

You have resolved that I shall not be and at all costs
You come towards me and in your haste
Laughing and weeping
You sweep
And destroy
All before you

You have resolved to destroy me at all costs
But you cannot find
The true path
To me

Because
You know the well-worn and the deep-cut paths
And no other
(And indeed they are narrow and barren
Moreover
For you
The strong and proud
They are hard
And
Long)
. . .

So you don't know that you are the least evil
Amongst my
Many
Great
Evils

You don't know who
You have to deal with

You know nothing about the map of my paths
You don't know that the path from you to me
Is not the same as the path
From me
To you

You know nothing about my riches
Hidden from your mighty eyes
(You don't know that
Much more
Than you think
Was turned
And

Given me
By Fate)

You have resolved to destroy me at all costs
But you cannot find the true path
To me
(I understand you:
You are a man in one space and time
Who lives only now and here
And knows nothing about the infinite
Space of time
In which I am
Present
From distant yesterday
Till distant tomorrow
Thinking
Of you

But that's not all)

—Mak Dizdar
Translated by Anne Pennington

8. Postmodernism's Relation to Evil

> By glorifying and blessing himself as his own creator, he commits the lie against being, yea, he wants to raise it, the lie, to rule over being—for truth shall no longer be what he experiences as such, but what he ordains as such.
>
> —Martin Buber

When addressing the significance of postmodernism, it is helpful to keep in mind that the founders of postmodernism—Michel Foucault, Jean-Francois Lyotard, and Jacques Derrida—are all admirers of the ancient Sophists. Foucault, for instance, identifies positively with Callicles in the *Gorgias* and Thrasymachus in the *Republic*. He resents the "reassuring dialectic" that Socrates employs to refute his ancient friends, and it is as if Foucault believes that, if he were to encounter Socrates today, he (unlike his ancient friends) would remain firm in his antipathy toward Platonic philosophy and defense of sophistry. Postmodernism is the serious revival and unabashed celebration of the Sophists' overturning of ancient philosophy.

With the publication of *A Journey to the Rivers: Justice for Serbia*, Peter Handke speaks about evil from a postmodern perspective. Shortly

---

An earlier version of this chapter appeared as "O nepravdi postmodernism: Peter Handke o Srbiji i lecija iz Bosne" in *Novi Izraz* and then in *Sociology after Bosnia and Kosovo: Recovering Justice*.

before the signing of the Dayton Peace Accord, Handke traveled to Belgrade and drove to the Drina River, thirty kilometers from the Srebrenica enclave, where five months earlier the Bosnian Serb Army and the Yugoslav People's Army methodically massacred approximately eight thousand men and sadistically abused women and children in this area that was declared by the United Nations to be a safe area. Why does Handke travel to Serbia and record his reflections?

> It was principally because of the war that I wanted to go to Serbia, into the country of the so-called aggressors. . . . Nearly all the photographs and reports of the last four years came from one side of the fronts or borders. When they occasionally came from the other side they seemed to me increasingly to be simply mirroring of the usual coordinated perspectives—distorted reflections in the very cells of our eyes and not eyewitness accounts. I felt the need to go behind the mirror; I felt the need to travel into the Serbia that became, with every article, every commentary, every analysis, less recognizable and more worthy of study, more worthy, simply of being seen. (1997, 2)

Handke opposes the one-sided news coverage of the war in Bosnia. The more commentary there is about Serbia, the less understood Serbia is. To counter this tendency in the global media, Handke wants to bear witness on behalf of the people of Serbia. He believes Serbia has the right "simply, of being seen."

What, though, do we get behind this mirror where journalistic representations no longer disfigure our vision? To give one example, Handke makes this observation:

> And on Serbian state television that farewell scene of President Milošević, immediately prior to his departure for the peace talks in Dayton, Ohio: walking down a long line of military and civilian people on the runway and hugging each one long and hard, the whole time visible only from the back—the departing man for long minutes only as a picture from the back. (1997, 37)

When Handke watches Milošević depart from Belgrade for Dayton, Ohio, what does he see? What do the people of Serbia see? At its best, Handke's narrative takes pictures. As few words as possible are connected with these pictures. As little discourse as necessary frames the photographs and their significance. Whatever meanings that are connected to the images appear random, and this notion of randomness holds the photograph and what it signifies together.

Walking on the Serbian bank of the Drina, Handke asks, "Was I being observed from the opposite bank? Nothing moved there in the ruins, or was it an unfinished building?" (1997, 37–38). What do we see in this picture? Perhaps a destroyed building; perhaps an unfinished house. Concretely speaking, who can say? With the truism of probability, Handke protects the people of Serbia from the righteous certitude of Western journalists. For Handke, meaning is never other than conditional. There are no absolutes, no innate meaningfulness within a picture. With the sword of skepticism, Handke protects the people of Serbia from the onslaught of the world's indignation. Such is the armor of righteous antirighteousness that Handke, the postmodern warrior, dons.

According to Handke, the problem with most accounts of the violence in Bosnia is that they are constructions disfigured by moral perspectives, and, according to Handke, these accounts are unconnected to the actuality of events. Handke reasons that violence is not always evil, nor are victims always innocent.

> Who can tell me I am mistaken or even malicious when, looking at the picture of the unrestrainedly crying face of a woman in close-up behind the bars of a prison camp, I see also the obedient following of directions given by the photographer of the international press agency outside the camp fence; and even in the way the woman clings to the wire I see something suggested by the picture merchant? (1997, 20–21)

In a way, Handke is right. The relationship between a photograph and its meaning, an image and its significance, a signifier and its signified, is never absolute or impregnable; like any discursive relationship, the photograph and its meaning are conditionally constructed and socially determined, and thus subject to skepticism.

Handke wants to teach his readers that there is never an authentic relationship between an image and its significance except the randomness of its construction. The picture of the unrestrainedly crying face of a woman does not necessarily reflect sincere grief or authentic sorrow. The truth that Handke heralds is that there never is an essential or integral relationship between a sign and what is signified. This is the notion of pragmatic intelligibility, which, according to Handke, is true for not only others' but also his own representations. Handke's advantage is simply that he embraces this postmodern epistemology that insists upon the randomness of what we assume we understand and disavows any principled character of discourse.

Consider Handke's own conduct at the public lectures following the publication of *A Journey to the Rivers: Justice for Serbia*, as reported in the media: "He adjusts his glasses, peers at the audience, and with nary a word of introduction, embarks on a 90-minute reading from his new book"; "In Frankfurt, a survivor of the concentration camp at Omarska asked to speak, and Handke angrily stormed out of the hall"; "In Vienna . . . when an individual in the hall rose to observe that Handke had never been in the war zone, whereas he, the speaker, had visited Sarajevo twenty times, Handke interrupted him: 'Then drive there for the twenty-first time, asshole!'" "When the man who translated six of Handke's books into Slovenian protested in an open letter that Handke was twisting the facts, Handke denied that the man was his translator" (Schneider 1997, 34–38). Where is Handke coming from? An aphorism from Walter Benjamin helps locate the foundation of Handke's acting out: "All efforts to render politics aesthetic culminate in one thing: war" (2004, 256).

One journalist who covered the war for *Der Spiegel* and who is a target of Handke's derision is Peter Schneider. Handke writes, "But what was my generation's response to Yugoslavia, . . . I know . . . mechanical scribbling, infatuated with images of enemies and war, collaborating instead of wall jumping, by the author Peter Schneider" (1997, 80–81). Handke sees Schneider's writing collaborating, collaborating with the Bosnian side; he sees Schneider employing moral dichotomies and demonizing one side. In contrast, Handke sees himself wall jumping.

Schneider, in his own review of Handke's book for the *New Republic*, says,

> I am not complaining that Handke is seeking to understand the Serbs, that he is demanding a more accurate view of them. When he forsakes the vanity of the heroic dissenter, when he is animated by a genuine curiosity about the landscape and the "people of Cain," Handke's book is an attempt to build a bridge between

enemies. But he dynamites his own bridge with his tirades, with his groundless, sweeping suspicions of all the critics of the Serbs. (1997, 36)

Handke wants to understand the Serbian people in an unfiltered way, and he takes exception to authors who are unwilling to understand Serbs on their own terms, who fail "simply, to see" the people in Serbia. We understand Handke's motive. We comprehend the conditions that provoke his conduct and the situation that centers it. However, what we need to consider carefully is the normative orientation that makes sense of the author, his motive, his conditions, his situation, and the value orientation that meaningfully holds these different elements together as action.

According to Handke, to understand the people of Serbia, one needs to become like the people of Serbia.

And how would I, as a Serb in Croatia, have related to such a state, established as an enemy to me and my people? Would I have emigrated "home" over the Danube to Serbia, although perhaps deeply bound to the place, in part by generations of ancestors? Perhaps. Would I, even if suddenly a second-class citizen, even if a coerced citizen of Croatia, have remained in the country, reluctantly to be sure, sad, full of gallows humor, but in the service of precious peace? Perhaps. Or, had it been in my power, would I have taken up arms—naturally, only with many others of my peers and, in an emergency, even with the help of a disintegrating, aimless Yugoslavian army? Probably, or, if I were, as such a Serb, halfway young and without a family of my own, almost certainly. (1997, 16)

Handke imagines himself as a Serb. He simulates what, according to him, it means to be a Serb. He transfers his projection of what a Serbian young man is onto himself and embodies it. Notice the escalating and final content of each progression: "Would I have taken up arms ... if I were, as such a Serb, halfway young and without a family of my own, almost certainly. And wasn't that how the war began, as is well known, with the marching of the first Croatian state militia into the Serbian villages around Vukovar?" (1997, 16). What would Handke have done during the war? Would he have taken up arms? Why would he have done so? Because he had nothing better to do. How did the war actually start? Did the destruction of Vukovar start spontaneously? No. Milošević's Belgrade regime carefully planned and ruthlessly executed the urbicide of Vukovar.

If Handke bears witness on behalf of the people of Serbia, how does he do so? What is the self-consciousness Handke ascribes to the Serbian people? Handke's particular mirroring of the Serbian self-consciousness resonates with the barbarian's rejection of the stranger. There is, Georg Simmel argues, a positive meaning in the expression, "the stranger." The stranger is a member of the group itself. The stranger is simultaneously familiar and remote, near and far, close and estranged. The expression "the stranger" indicates how differences are preserved but not encompassed, cherished but not collapsed in modern societies.

The barbarian, though, is intolerant of the stranger.

> The relation of the Greeks to the barbarians is a typical example; so are all the cases in which the general characteristics one takes as peculiarly and merely human are disallowed to the other. But here the expression "the stranger" no longer has any positive meaning. The relation with him is a non-relation. (Simmel 1950, 407)

For the barbarian, there is no relation to the stranger. To the stranger, the barbarian says, "We cannot live together." When the stranger is a member of the group, the barbarian's rejection of the stranger is violent. The more the stranger is a familiar member of the group, the more violent the barbarian's rejection. The barbarian's prejudice disallows to the stranger "the general characteristics one takes as peculiarly and merely human" (Simmel 1950, 407).

Let us take an example directly from Handke's writing: "How, my immediate thought had been, is that ever supposed to end well, the high-handed establishment of a state by a single people—if the Serbo-Croatian-speaking Muslim descendants of Serbs in Bosnia are in fact a people—in a region to which two other peoples have a right, and the same right!" Handke's conditional phrase, "If the Serbo-Croatian-speaking Muslim descendants of Serbs in Bosnia are in fact a people," rejects the cultural identity of Bosnian Muslims and denies the history of Bosnians. Handke negates the historical principle that Bosnian Muslims as well as Bosnians are distinctive. While it is true that the history of Bosnians is intertwined with the history of Serbs and Croats, the history of Bosnians is also specific and unique. Only after Bosnia became a part of the Ottoman Empire in the late fourteenth century did the Orthodox Church begin to establish a meaningful presence in the interior of Bosnia. The Orthodox Church was more favored than the Catholic Church. For the next four hundred years, the Orthodox Church grew in number within Bosnia while the more oppressed Catholic Church, given its relation to Rome, declined. Paradoxically, if it had not been for Ottoman rule, the Orthodox Church would not have established a significant presence within the interior of Bosnia (Hastings 1994, Donia and Fine 1994, Malcolm 1994).

Notice not only the historical inaccuracy but also the false logic that undergirds Handke's statement: "If the Serbo-Croatian-speaking Muslim descendants of Serbs in Bosnia are in fact a people" (1997, 18). If, on the one hand, Bosnian Muslims are distinct from Serbs, they have no relation to them. If, on the other hand, Bosnian Muslims are not distinct from Serbs, they are the same as them. They are derivative and do not exist as Bosnian Muslims. Here is the perverse logic that animated Serb propaganda and the twisted ideology that guided its sociocidal activities against Bosnia. Handke not only hears; he also parrots.

How does Handke's postmodern travelogue through Serbia help us understand evil? Taking another picture, Handke writes the following:

> In the main hall of the bus station, the destination board, as large as a monumental painting. Here the Cyrillic letters I had grown accustomed to felt like calligraphy: БЕОГРАД (Beograd) and under it, at the end, СРЕБРЕНИЦА and ТУЗЛА (Srebrenica and Tuzla). This tremendous and seemingly ancient board, however, was no longer valid. The current timetable had been pasted over a corner, a tiny, formlessly lettered piece of paper, and there were, for the two last-named places as well as others, no more departures. (1997, 71–72)

From Handke's point of view, this lonely destination board in the main hall of the bus station is no longer valid. But why? Five months before his travels to the area, members of the society called Yugoslavia (i.e., the Serbo-Croatian-speaking Muslims who lived in Srebrenica and Tuzla) were grotesquely and unconscionably assaulted. Nationalist Serbs drove "these strangers" out of their homes and communities with unconscionable terror; they sadistically murdered many. How ancient then is this Serbian destination board at the bus station with the destinations of Srebrenica and Tuzla in Cyrillic letters? What culture, what values, what normative orientation did this monumental painting positively represent? Handke takes enigmatic pictures; he takes pictures randomly, feeding parasitically off the positive meaning of the images that his prosaic camera indifferently captures. As an artist, Handke deepens evil's negativity.

There is one image in Handke's travelogue, however, whose significance is not random, and this image is the Drina. The Drina is the guiding trope of Handke's narrative.

> And I squatted down there, which made the river stretch a little wider, nothing now from the tips of my Serbian winter shoes to the Bosnian bank except the water of the Drina, smoky cold. . . . Downriver, perhaps fewer than thirty kilometers, began, apparently, the region of the Srebrenica enclave. A child's sandal broke the surface at my feet. (1997, 73)

What now links Handke's Serbian winter boots with the Bosnian shore? Nothing. Nothing except the cold water of the Drina. Handke is not, as Schneider naively suggests, trying to build a bridge between enemies. If Handke were, standing there on the Serbian side of the Drina is where he would begin to build such a bridge. "A child's sandal broke the surface at my feet." Why did Handke not pick up the child's sandal? Why did he not ask where the child's sandal came from? Why did he not ask where the child is now? Handke allows the image to float by him and sink into the dark, smoky waters of indefinite possibilities.

For a brief moment, Handke does cross the Drina over to Bosnia. Before turning back, here is what he reports, "The border guard with the eyes of a sniper—or wasn't it rather a kind of incurable, inaccessible sadness? Only a god could have relieved him of it, and in my eyes the empty, dark Drina flowed past as such a god, if a completely powerless one" (1997, 60). In Handke's narrative, the Drina is an image whose significance is authentic. The Drina is the ineffable muse from whom he discovers no foundation upon which to build a bridge between Bosnia and Serbia. This is the point of his book. For Handke, the Drina represents a postmodern god, a living, metaphysical, bottomless, impotent chasm, over whose waters it is impossible to build a bridge between Bosnia and Serbia despite the fact that such bridges exist historically and symbolically. Even postmodern prophets lapse into grand metanarratives, grand narratives whose import is at the same time critically admonished by them as oppressively totalizing. Handke is human; he, too, needs order and not just the order of disorder. What, then, is the nature of this order?

Handke admires the self-consciousness of the Serbian people, and he believes that they live closer to reality with all its rawness. Today, the Serbian people live in a situation quite close to a Hobbesian jungle where the randomness of force and fraud and the inconsistency of untempered self-interest are the normative orientations guiding society. Yes, an order exists in Serbia, but it is simply a factual order. It is not truly a normative order, and this fact becomes the dysfunctional normative order for Serbia today. Talcott Parsons explains this paradox and the problem it presents: "Thus a social order is always a factual order in so far as it is susceptible of scientific analysis but, as will be later maintained, it is one which cannot have stability without the effective functioning of certain normative elements" (1968, 92). How long can the Serbian people sustain themselves and their community without the effective functioning of certain normative elements? Can society have stability when normative values such as "Thou Shall Not Murder," "Thou Shall Not Steal, "Thou Shall Not Bear False Witness," or "Thou Shall Not Covet Thy Neighbor's Wife" seem nonexistent in the community? Serbia has become an experiment in postmodern social theory.

What principle of justice does Handke then see himself bringing the people of Serbia? Handke recounts a striking event in Belgrade, and his narration of it shows the degree to which he is riveted to his subject:

> A kind of panel discussion was now supposed to take place about general conditions, about the Bosnian war, about the Bosnian Serbia, Serbian Serbia role in the war. For a long time we sat in near silence, edgy, at a loss, with a huge bottle of Frascati, and an ancient one at that. . . . And then gradually, as a matter of course, the subject changed to contemporary Yugoslavia. One man in the room finally literally screamed at how guilty the Serbia leaders were for the present suffering of their people, from the oppression of the Albanians in Kosovo to the thoughtless recognition of the Krajina Republic. It was an outcry, not an expression of opinion, not simply an oppositional voice from a cultural gathering in a dark room. (1997, 48–49)

Handke has trouble tolerating this stranger. When the man speaks, Handke hears a cry expressing no opinion. He hears the sound of an animal rather than the voice of a human being. For Handke, if conditions are such that to speak one can only sound like a voiceless animal, the decision that preserves one's humanity is silence. This man failed Handke's criteria of what would preserve his humanity. Why? "And this Serb spoke only about his own leaders; the war dogs elsewhere were spared, as if their deeds themselves screamed to heaven, or to somewhere else" (1997, 50). For Handke, the man's words (no matter how valid and compelling) carry no weight because they are only about Serbian leaders and not about the other war dogs. This is the barbaric logic behind Handke's critique: one must speak first negatively of "them" and then positively about "us." Loyalty is demonstrated by never speaking negatively about "us." Handke does not only witness this rule of loyalty; he polices it.

In Handke's report on his meeting with others, however, we hear of a voice that resists. From a moral point of view, this event at a panel discussion is heartening. We are not interested in the self-consciousness of the Serbian people, however cosmopolitan it may be; instead, we are interested in the conscience of the Serbian people. The reason Handke finds the Serbian people "overly self-conscious" is because the gap between their self-consciousness and their conscience is great. Evil creates a chasm between a community's self-consciousness and conscience. "Only a god could have relieved him of it, and in my eyes the empty, dark Drina flowed past as such a god, if a completely powerless one" (1997, 60). The greater the chasm, the greater the dissonance, which becomes itself a perverted form of conscience. For Handke, the Drina symbolizes this chasm that he witnesses; the Drina symbolizes not evil directly, but the consequence of evil.

Handke rejects the man who speaks up, the man who demonstrates a positive relation between his self-consciousness and his conscience. He rejects the man who resists evil. Handke rejects, as well, the part of himself that identifies with this man:

> Strange, however: although in this man's presence I finally lost my sense that anything was official or calculated about the situation—rather than making statements, he suffered, angrily and transparently—I did not want to hear his damnation of his leaders; not here, in this space, nor in the city or the country; and not

now, when a peace was perhaps in the works, after a war that had been started and finally probably decided with the help of foreign, utterly different powers. (That he then hugged me as we parted was, I thought there, because he felt understood, and I ask myself now whether his motivation wasn't rather that he hadn't.) (1997, 50)

When this man courageously abandons the role of voiceless barbarian, Handke suffocates him with the nationalistic rhetoric from which the man wishes to escape. He disallows the man "the general characteristics one takes as peculiarly and merely human" (Simmel 1950, 407). Handke returns the man to the void in which the man objects to having been placed. In this interaction, Handke refuses to see an authentic human being living in an inauthentic community. Handke restipulates the barbarian's oppressive line of reasoning: the Serbian leaders are not the ones who started the war; the war was started by foreign powers, foreign powers that are "utterly different."

It is important not to treat Handke in the same way that he treats the man who speaks up. It is important to hear Handke justly. To do so, it is important to ask what version of justice Handke sees himself promoting. Every person sees their actions aiming at some good. Toward what good does Hanke see his deeds aim? Handke poses the question, the question that links his self-consciousness and his conscience:

> Didn't my generation fail to grow up during the wars in Yugoslavia? . . . In what way? . . . What was my generation's response to Yugoslavia, in the case that was for us . . . of earth-shattering importance . . . from those of my approximate age, I know. . . . Peter Schneider, arguing for the intervention of NATO against the criminal Bosno-Serbs. . . . To grow up, to do justice to, to not only embody a reaction to the century's night and thus add to the darkening, but to break out of this night. (1997, 80–81)

For Handke, justice not only embodies, but also breaks out of the century's night. According to Handke, a NATO intervention against the criminal Bosno-Serbs is merely a reaction to the century's night; it only adds to the darkening. A NATO intervention begets an action that is another use of force, equal in kind to the force against which it reacts, equally criminal. For Handke, a NATO intervention ignores what Max Weber refers to as the ethical irrationality of the world (Weber 1958,

123). Handke equates just action on behalf of the hundreds of thousands of victims in Bosnia with unfair consequences for the criminal Bosno-Serbs. This intellectualizing line was heard often during the war.

The principle of justice that Handke denies is justice not only for the victims, but also for the wrongdoers. In *Gorgias*, Socrates identifies the logic that Handke rebuffs.

> *Socrates*: Will a man who does wrong be happy if he is brought to justice and punished?
> *Polus*: On the contrary, he will then be most miserable.
> *Socrates*: But, by your account, if he isn't brought to justice he will be happy?
> *Polus*: Yes.
> *Socrates*: On the other hand, Polus, my opinion is that the wicked man and the doer of wicked acts is miserable in any case, but more miserable if he does not pay the penalty and suffer punishment for his crimes, and less miserable if he does pay the penalty and suffer punishment in this world.
> *Polus*: What an extraordinary proposition to maintain, Socrates.
>
> (Plato 1960, 59)

Is bringing justice to bear on the criminal Bosno-Serbs advantageous only to their victims? According to Socrates, bringing justice to bear on the doers of wicked acts is also advantageous to the doers of wicked acts. It brings the light of fairness and dignity not only to the hundreds of thousands of victims in Bosnia, but also to their victimizers. Justice restores the shredded relation between the victimizers' self-consciousness and conscience. Justice, moreover, allows the victims to sustain their relation between their self-consciousness and conscience so as to avoid falling into the same chasm as their victimizers. The restoration is advantageous to the community within which both the victims and victimizers live. This and only this creates the possibility of reintegration; tragically, Bosnians still wait for this imperative.

Like Polus, Handke argues that bringing justice to bear on the criminal Bosno-Serbs would be in itself another injustice. To some degree, this logic grounds the actions of European and American leaders toward the criminal Bosno-Serbs who still remain free, Ratko Mladić and Radovan Karadžić. Handke's postmodern reasoning is that preserving a nonrelation between one's self-consciousness and one's conscience is a natural right. To accept such reasoning, one must believe, like Polus at this moment in the dialogue, that bringing justice to bear on wrongdoers would make wrongdoers more miserable. One must believe that the doers of wicked acts would be more happy if they escaped punishment and less happy if they were punished. Furthermore, one must believe that the greater the injustice, the greater the misery for the wrongdoer if brought to justice. Thus, someone responsible for the consequences of sociocide will experience the greatest misery imaginable if brought to justice. Socrates argues that this position is morally as well as empirically false.

Allowing the criminal Bosno-Serbs to maintain a nonrelation between their self-consciousness and conscience is not in the interest of the criminal Bosno-Serbs. The greater the gap between their self-consciousness and conscience, the greater their unhappiness. It is hard to imagine a pain greater than not being brought to justice for planning and ordering the rapes and murders of hundreds of thousands of human beings who were neighbors, friends, and relatives. It is unconscionable to leave human beings responsible for such horrific crimes in this state; it is an affront to humanity, both theirs and ours.

If, in turn, the victims of war crimes are asked to forget the evil that they experienced, they are asked to adapt the same nonrelation between their self-consciousness and their conscience as their victimizers. Some European and American political leaders seem to reason "why perpetuate the cycle of pain." They suggest that someone must stop the cycle, even if the point at which it is stopped randomly and conditionally favors the unjust. Their solution is that, for victims to preserve their sanity, their choice must be to adapt the same nonrelation between their self-consciousness and their conscience as their victimizers. This nonrelation is the hallmark of not only evil but also madness.

This shielding action toward war criminals like Mladić and Karadžić is based on a self-defeating representation of natural right. Ten years after the genocide in Srebrenica, Mladić is still negotiating his possible surrender, asking for financial security for his family and amnesty for those who sheltered him. In Plato's *Gorgias*, Callicles says to Socrates, "I tell you frankly that natural good and right consist in this, that the man who is going to live as a man ought should encourage his appetites to be as strong as possible instead of repressing them, and be able by means of his courage and intelligence to satisfy them in all their intensity by providing them with whatever they happen to desire" (1960, 90). From the perspective of this notion of natural right, which is the normative framework within which evil reveals itself, it is more base to suffer wrong than to do wrong, to be murdered than to murder, and to be raped than to rape. From this normative framework, before suffering wrong, it is better to do wrong. In public speeches, Karadžić used this normative framework with the Serbian people to start a murderous campaign of terror against Bosnians and, more specifically, Bosnian Muslims.

Morality, however, is the knowledge that it is more base to do wrong than to suffer wrong, to be a murderer than to be murdered, and to be a rapist than to be raped. This recognition establishes a normative order that is not just a factual order. This recognition establishes a bridge between self-consciousness and conscience; it provides a bridge over which every member of the community traverses.

What would be a moral response "on the part of our generation to Yugoslavia"? Handke poses the question, but does not answer it. A moral response recognizes the need of the Serbian people to overcome the nonrelation between their self-consciousness and their conscience. What triggered the repetition of the grotesque and immense Serbian violence against Albanians in Kosovo in 1999? Such horrific events were triggered by the gap between the self-consciousness and the conscience of the Serbian people. The violence agaist Kosovo was a cry of pain on the part of the Serbian people. The reason for the cry of pain was the seemingly unbridgeable chasm between their self-consciousness and their conscience. The Serbian people cannot do what they must do to become a community without a stable normative order; they cannot bring justice to bear upon themselves. They do not know how to bridge their self-consciousness and their conscience. The violence in Kosovo was a perverse way that the Serbian people attempted to force others to do for the Serbian people what the Serbian people could no longer do for themselves.

A moral response intervenes in the face of evil not only on behalf of the hundreds of thousands of victims, but also on behalf of those guilty of crimes against humanity. A moral response awakens the sleeping conscience of the guilty and begins to soothe their sleepless nights.

"Neither the man who establishes a dictatorship by crime nor the man who is punished for attempting to do so can ever be described as the happier; you can't compare the happiness of two people who are both miserable. But the man who gets away with it and becomes a dictator is the more miserable. What's this, Polus? Laughing?" (Plato 1960, 61).

9. Psychologizing Evil

After the massacre at Srebrenica in 1995, General Mladić—the chief perpetrator—said triumphantly, "Everything that happened here happened under the eyes of the world."

—Alan Little

People in Bosnia were victimized by aggression from Serbia and Croatia and by criminal elements within their own country; they were also victimized by the world's nonunderstanding of this evil. Even though media accounts attempted to explain the motivation behind the destruction of so many lives, families, and communities, they often fell short.

There is, however, preexisting literature that explains the evil that the people of Bosnia-Herzegovina suffered. One such essay is titled "On Nationalism" by Danilo Kiš. The essay has been reprinted in two anthologies, *Why Bosnia?* (Ali and Lifschultz 1993) and *Scar on the Stone* (Agee 1998). It is too late to change what happened to the people of Bosnia; it is not, however, too late to revisit this notable essay and show its continued relevance. Such a review could resist a repetition of evil under the guise of nationalism not only in Bosnia but also elsewhere in the world.

An earlier version of this chapter appeared in *Sociologija nakon Bosne* and as "O upotrebi dvoličnog diskursa u globalnim medijima od strane počinitelja ratnih zločina u Bosni [On the double-voiced discourse in the global media by perpetrators of war crimes in Bosnia]" in *Odjek*.

Drawing upon Jean-Paul Sartre's analysis (1965) of anti-Semitism in his *Anti-Semite and Jew*, Kiš formulates the self-concept of the nationalist in Yugoslavia. Kiš shows how the anti-Semite in France and the nationalist in former-Yugoslavia share a similar pathology. Kiš makes an underappreciated point: while the nationalist has a consciousness (which is fantastical and enigmatic), the nationalist lacks an *individual* consciousness. Persons whose selves exemplify an individual consciousness are both feared and held in contempt, especially if they are from the nationalist's own community.

Kiš makes several telling points on the shallow psychology of nationalists, but his most pressing point is this one, regarding the nationalist's lack of *individuality*.

> If, in the framework of a social order, an individual is not able to "express himself," because the order in question is not congenial and does not stimulate him as an *individual*, or because it thwarts him as an individual, in other words does not allow him to assume an entity of his own, he is obliged to search for this entity outside identity and outside the so-called social structure. (1993, 126)

In terms of social psychology, the matter is difficult. If the individual searches for his or her consciousness outside of identity and outside of the so-called social structure, where does the individual find this consciousness? There is a metaphysical answer to this question. The *soul* is the nonempirical foundation for the individual's consciousness. Martin Buber (1958) speaks to and of the soul through the notion of the I–Thou relation in contrast to the empirical I–It relation. The I–Thou relation is not an idealized principle for Buber; it is a reality that exists in the individual's relation to nature, other human beings, society, and God.

There is also an empirical answer to this question of with what resources outside of identity and the social structure the individual develops his or her own consciousness. George Herbert Mead (1934) formulates the concept of the self's "me" and the self's "I." The "me" is the socialized character of the individual that is developed through the self's capacity to take the role of the other in social interaction, whether that other is an individual or, more broadly, the generalized other of the community. The Golden Rule, "Do unto others as you would have them do unto you," is an adage recommending role-taking with another. The Golden Rule states the ethos of goodwill, that is, it concretely and pragmatically identifies a universal understanding of the attitude of the generalized other.

In contrast to the self's "me," the self's "I" is the unique and distinctive nature of the self, that aspect that is representative of the individual per se vis-à-vis the individual's relations to others. Inevitably, the self's "me" encompasses the self's "I," but never completely; if the self's "me" did, the result would be an authoritarian personality. The result would be an individual with no sense of distinctiveness and individuality, whose consciousness would be derived totally from the self's ability to conform to and take the role of an authoritarian figure to which the self is subject. The individual would have no *individual* consciousness.

For Mead, a sense of one's own *individuality* is constructed through neither the dominance of the "me" over the "I" nor the dominance of the "I" over the "me," but through the dialogical relation of the "me" and the "I." Self-consciousness is the mutual awareness that the self's "me" and the self's "I" have of each other. An individual consciousness is based on the relation between these two parts of the self and the history of this relation.

Conscience, as opposed to self-consciousness, is twofold; it is the "I" accepting the "me" and the "me's" relation to the generalized other that is society. It is also the "me" accepting the self's "I" as the part of the self that yearns for a sense of individuality and the principle of authentic freedom.

The self of the nationalist doubts the possibility of an *individual* consciousness and abandons this ambition from which no self can ever entirely free itself. Kiš cites several passages from Sartre. For instance, the anti-Semite, Sartre says, has no inner self with which to see its self.

> He is not afraid of himself, but he sees in the eyes of others a disquieting image—his own—and he makes his words and gestures conform to it. Having this external model, he is under no necessity to look for his personality within himself. He has chosen to find his being entirely outside himself, never to look within, to be nothing save the fear he inspires in others. What he flees even more than Reason is his intimate awareness of himself. (1965, 21)

In his description of the Bosnian Serb nationalist leader, Radovan Karadžić, Semezdin Mehmedinović provides an example.

Karadžić came across as a peace-loving and good-natured fellow. During the first multi-party elections, after the fall of socialism, he founded the Greens. That seemed quite in character. Founding such a party, given conditions in the Balkans, was more like an artistic performance than true political engagement. The Greens' first political action in Sarajevo proved this: They draped plastic bags in various colours over the boughs of the acacias lining some of Sarajevo's main streets.

Not long after this Radovan became the leader of the Serb nationalists. In order to fit his new role, he deliberately held his left hand off to the side so that inquisitive onlookers could see the handle of a pistol tucked under his jacket. (1998, 83)

The shift from being a founder of the Greens Party, an antimilitaristic group, to being a charismatic leader of the Serbian nationalists, who viciously destroyed Bosnia, is hard to grasp. There are many journalistic accounts of Karadžić, but none record this odd shift. The shift is telltale when we refer to Kiš's account of nationalism. What do the Greens Party and Serbian Democratic Party have in common such that one person could be the political leader of both groups? The shift exposes something notable about Karadžić. At one point, he is directed by the image of himself that he sees in the eyes of the Greens Party; at another point, he is directed by the image of himself that he sees in the eyes of the nationalist Serbian Democratic Party. Embarrassment, if we understand Mead, requires a sense of individuality; it is the self's recognition of its self in a social context. Self witnesses its self's discordance with its social environment. Embarrassment reveals self's self-consciousness. When a person blushes, we witness the person's "I" and the person's "me" out of harmony. We also witness the person's "I" and the person's "me" recognizing themselves in relation to one another. This is self-consciousness. When the child blushes when the mother catches its hand in the cookie jar, the child's "me" (taking the role of the mother as the mother sees the child with its hand in the cookie jar) and the child's "I" (the desire to have a cookie before lunch) recognize themselves as one and as discordant. The child's "self" is caught not only by the mother's recognition of its self but also by its own recognition of its self. The child does not cower in fear; the child blushes. The blush is a physical representation of an individual self-consciousness.

Shamelessness, that is, the incapacity to be embarrassed, is the incapacity of the self's "me" and the self's "I" to recognize themselves in relation to each other. Shamelessness reflects a consciousness that lacks a sense of individuality. This point inverts the conventional understanding of Karadžić. During the aggression against Bosnia-Herzegovina, diplomats often described Karadžić as entirely inner-directed. They suggested that he was so inner-directed that he was incorrigible, impossible to negotiate with. It was impossible, they said, to stop him from realizing his ambitions, however perverse and demented they were. Yasushi Akashi, the UN special envoy to former Yugoslavia, was asked, "About Karadžić: Can you give an example of something he said or thought that surprised you?" Akashi responded,

> He is a man of the past, captivated by history and the glory of the Serbian nation. I tried to direct his eyes to the future, to the outer world, to the consequences of his military actions. But he is a headstrong man. Some Bosnian Serbs are almost suicidal, comparable to the Massad psychology [named after the rock where Jewish rebels in A.D. 73 chose to commit suicide rather than surrender to the Romans]. It is impossible to penetrate their minds. I told them: you are a minority, condemned and isolated by the international community. But they did not care. (Van de Roer 1998)

Mehmedinović would make the opposite point. He would say that Karadžić is neither headstrong nor inner-directed. On the one hand, Akashi says that Karadžić is opaque; it is impossible to penetrate the man's mind. On the other hand, Mehmedinović says that Karadžić is transparent; he lacks a sense of individuality.

One observes this matter indirectly in the odd interactions between Karadžić and others in the BBC documentary *Serbian Epics* directed by Pawel Pawlikowski. In one scene with his mother in Montenegro, Karadžić is the doting son seeking a distant mother's approval. In another, he is the fatalistic poet on the mountains above Sarajevo pointing out where he once lived during the murderous shelling he is directing. In yet another, he is playing the gusle, singing ballads in the birthplace of his namesake, Serbian linguist Vuc Karadžić.

In each scene, it is as if Karadžić is on the verge of blushing, but, in fact, he is unable to blush. His "me," his capacity to take the role of the other, functions. What does not function is his capacity to take the role of another so as to see himself through the eyes of another. Mehmedinović writes,

> Lies were the only political means in which Radovan Karadžić had absolute faith. Since everything he did in the name of racial "cleanliness" created a fact, so to speak—all he had left to do was keep repeating the lies until his accumulated acts made his lies seem irrefutable. (1998, 21)

Some Western politicians began to accept and endorse Karadžić's racist pronouncements that Bosnians could not live together. The longer Western diplomats allowed Karadžić to persist with his lies, the longer Karadžić had to create not only the normative orientation but also the factual reality that supported his mendacity. The longer Karadžić had to establish an apartheid infrastructure through war crimes and crimes against humanity, the longer he had to make his outsider's notion that Bosnians could not live together—a fait accompli.

Notice a paradox. The media directly contributes to the creation of Karadžić's maniacal self. If through his observation of others' observations of him Karadžić sees an individual who is inner-directed and invincible, Karadžić understands himself as inner-directed and invincible. Karadžić actively solicited the media's attention and then took his bearings from it. Karadžić was fixated on others' perceptions of him because they were his sole source of self-knowledge. Karadžić had no individual consciousness. He was incapable of recognizing himself himself.

This paradox reveals the way in which Karadžić sustained his legitimacy among nationalist Serbs and also within the international community. Karadžić's legitimacy was not traditional, not legal, not democratic, and not rational; it was and still is charismatic. Posters in the major cities of Serbia and Republika Srpska still proclaim "Every Serb is Radovan." During the war, Karadžić's legitimacy was superior to other forms of legitimacy simply because the unjust war could not be stopped. Karadžić needed the war and needed it to be as unjust as possible in order to maintain his charismatic legitimacy.

It is helpful to refer to Max Weber's writing on this point.

> The charismatic leader gains and maintains authority solely by proving his strength in life. . . . The genuinely charismatic ruler is responsible precisely to those whom he rules. (1958, 248)

Karadžić's charisma trumped international law, local traditions, democratic processes, and rational persuasion. Ten years after the war, Karadžić continues to show his strength in life with people living in Republika Srpska by still avoiding capture. The inability and unwillingness of Western leaders and military police to arrest Karadžić for his war crimes and crimes against humanity compel Bosnian Serbs in Republika Srpska to acknowledge Karadžić as their leader. Note again Weber on this matter.

> The holder of charisma seizes the task that is adequate for him and demands obedience and a following by virtue of his mission. His success determines whether he finds them. His charismatic claim breaks down if his mission is not recognized by those to whom he feels he has been sent. If they recognize him, he is their master—so long as he knows how to maintain recognition through "proving" himself. (1958, 248–49)

Nothing else empowers Karadžić as much as the international community's failure to arrest him, and thus the international community is itself directly responsible for empowering Karadžić. Karadžić needs the international community's ineffective attempts to arrest him to maintain his charismatic authority. It is absurd as well as insulting for international diplomats to ask and expect Bosnian Serbs to arrest Karadžić when the actions of the Western powers themselves make such a feat impossible for Bosnian Serbs. The inability of Western leaders themselves to apprehend Karadžić contributes to Karadžić's aura of invincibility among his own people. This, in turn, makes it impossible for Bosnian Serbs to apprehend Karadžić. Bosnian Serbs are forced to follow Karadžić because he continues to prove to his enslaved followers his invincible strength. Asking the Bosnian Serbs to arrest him is yet only another sign of weakness in the eyes of the Bosnian Serbs, a sign of weakness that empowers Karadžić and forces Bosnian Serbs to remain loyal to their unwanted but immovable leader.

However, once one recognizes that as a charismatic figure Karadžić is as other-directed as he is and how he lacks an individual consciousness, one begins to see how vulnerable he truly is. Charismatic leaders maintain power only through being recognized, and Western leaders and diplomats, unwittingly or not, collude with Karadžić in this regard. Karadžić could not be as powerful as he is without the complicity, intentional or not, of the international community. By avoiding arrest in

Republika Srpska, especially after the arrest of Slobodan Milošević in Belgrade, Karadžić maintains charismatic legitimacy within Republika Srpska and, by implication, the state of Bosnia-Herzegovina. This form of legitimacy, because of its spectacular and extraordinary character, trumps other types of political legitimacy such as traditional authority, legal authority, rational authority, and even utilitarian authority.

Once we recognize that the basis of power for a charismatic leader is his ability to take his bearings directly from his followers, it is easy to undermine this power base. International law or signed agreements do not work. References to traditional Bosnian norms do not work and neither do rational refutations. Only shame works because shame induces an individual consciousness. One needs to hold up a mirror to not only the charismatic leader, but also his followers. One needs to hold up a mirror that forces Karadžić's "me" and Karadžić's "I" to reconnect so that the connection between his self-consciousness and his conscience reappears to his self. The categorical commitment to the principle of justice is the essence of this mirror. The charismatic leader and his followers need to see in this mirror their reflection in order to awaken their individual consciousnesses, in order to blush.

Failure goes a long way to undermine the power base of a charismatic leader if only because with failure the leader is no longer able to prove himself to his followers and is no longer able to demand his followers' obedience. Since the charismatic leader lacks a sense of individuality, the leader cannot come to terms with such failure and its political consequences. The charismatic leader is a prisoner as well; he is a prisoner of the need to succeed stupendously in the eyes of the people who revere him. Karadžić is as entrapped as the people over whom he dominates. Any failure on his part as a charismatic leader emancipates the people subject to his tyranny. Since charismatic authority lives so parasitically off of social admiration, charismatic authority is the weakest form of legitimacy, no matter how sensational it may be. This is why the NATO bombings, however limited and brief, were so quickly effective in changing Karadžić's behavior and bringing the war to a halt.

What then is the reason for the world's nonunderstanding of evil? Is the reason a comparable lack of individual consciousness among those observing the war crimes and crimes against humanity in Bosnia-Herzegovina? Is a consequence of watching the injustice against people in

Bosnia-Herzegovina a lack of an individual consciousness among people throughout the world?

At the start of this chapter, we asked with what resources the self establishes its individual consciousness, considering both the metaphysical and the empirical answer. Kiš says that the nationalist is obliged to find these resources outside identity and outside the social structure. How, though, can an individual find its individual consciousness outside of these resources? Note a problem in Mead's theorizing on this matter.

> The individual experiences himself as such, not directly, but only indirectly, from the particular standpoints of other individual members of the same social group, or from the generalized standpoint of the social group as a whole to which he belongs. For he enters his own experience as a self or individual, not directly or immediately, not by becoming a subject to himself, but only insofar as he first becomes an object to himself just as other individuals are objects to him or in his experience; and he becomes an object to himself only by taking the attitudes of other individuals toward himself within a social environment or context of experience and behavior in which both he and they are involved. (1934, 125)

Note in Mead's writing the secondary and devalued notion of what an individual consciousness is. The idea of being a subject to oneself, of having an individual consciousness through which one knows oneself directly, is the negative and contrasting idea to Mead's theorizing on the self. What, therefore, is rejected in Mead's theorizing is the possibility of knowing the self directly, of becoming a subject to oneself immediately. The work of the Russian psychologist Lev Vygotsky poignantly recovers Mead's dismissed notion and reformulates it strongly, "The inner speech of the adult represents his 'thinking for himself' rather than social adaptation" (1962, 18).

The solution to this problem is to bridge the gap between empiricism and metaphysics. Mead chooses not to when he writes, "I do not mean to raise the metaphysical question of how a person can be both 'I' and 'me' but to ask for the significance of this distinction from the point of view of conduct itself" (1956, 229). Everything in Mead's social psychology, however, brings us to this metaphysical question, which, as Mead demonstrates, is both empirical and nonempirical. The answer is found in what we speak of as conscience as opposed to self-consciousness.

Charismatic leaders are what is known in social psychology as high self-monitors; both Kiš and Sartre suggest this point. In *Public Appearances, Private Realities: The Psychology of Self-Monitoring*, Mark Snyder writes,

> The prototype of the high self-monitor is someone who is particularly sensitive to cues to the situational appropriateness of his or her social behavior and who uses these cues as guidelines for monitoring (that is, regulating and controlling) his or her expressive behavior and self-presentations. By contrast, the low self-monitor is less attentive to social information about situationally appropriate self-presentation and does not possess a highly developed repertoire of self-presentation skills. (1987, 13)

Consider the infamous utterance of Ratko Mladić upon the capture of the UN-declared safe haven, Srebrenica, and the slaughter of thousands of men, as well as the murders and rapes of numerous women and children. If Mladić were so inner-directed, why would he ask and insist upon being accompanied by a television crew the minute he enters Srebrenica and why would he choose to say at this moment, "We present this city to the Serbian people as a gift"? Why was it necessary for Mladić to conduct himself in this way? Speaking to the television camera after entering Srebrenica, Mladić said, "Finally, after the rebellion of the Dahis, the time has come to take revenge on the Turks in this region."

Mladić is a high self-monitor who is "particularly sensitive to cues to the situational appropriateness of his or her social behavior and who uses these cues as guidelines for monitoring (that is, regulating and controlling) his or her expressive behavior and self-presentations" (Synder 1987, 13). On the one hand, there is the unspeakable obscenity of this war crime and the long list of crimes against humanity over several years, a record that culminated in this grotesque event. On the other hand, Mladić feels called upon to present what is happening in Srebrenica immediately and directly and reveal his responsibility for it in the most favorable light possible to the Serbian people. As Mladić himself proclaimed, "Everything that happened here happened under the eyes of the world" (Little 2001). This variable was a decisive feature of

Mladić's evil. Mladić feels compelled to make this performative statement because he is so other-directed that he has no individual consciousness. He "sees in the eyes of others a disquieting image—his own—and he makes his words and gestures conform to it. Having this external model, he is under no necessity to look for his personality within himself" (Sartre 1965, 21)

The grotesque gift that Mladić presents to the Serbian people is now a curse for them that not even the Serbian Orthodox Church can sufficently mask. Mladić hopes that the Serbian people and he may together share the curse and remain eternally bonded. Until the Serbian people disassociate themselves from this gift, until the Serbian people view Mladić in a noncharismatic light, until the Serbian people hold up a mirror in which Mladić as well as they see their true reflection, this gift, "this revenge against the Turks after the rebellion of the Dahis" will curse the Serbian people throughout history.

10. RITUALIZING EVIL

> Herein lies the principle of Evil, not in some mystical agency or transcendence, but as a concealment of the symbolic order.
>
> —Jean Baudrillard

There are many books written on Bosnia and the Balkans from historical, political, journalistic, philosophical, and sociological points of view. One such book is Maria Todorova's *Imagining the Balkans*. It is worthwhile looking closely at Todorova's concluding sentence. While an author's last words are often the most enigmatic, they can also be the most revealing:

> If Europe has produced not only racism but also antiracism, not only misogyny but also feminism, not only anti-Semitism, but also its repudiation, then what can be termed Balkanism has not yet been coupled with its complementing and ennobling antiparticle. (1997, 189)

There are problems with this concluding sentence. One is that Balkanism is correlated with racism, misogyny, and anti-Semitism. The correlation is unduly negative. Racism evokes hatred, misogyny,

---

Portions of this chapter were presented as a lecture, "The Politics of Scapegoating: A Critique for the Sake of Democracy in Southeastern Europe" at the Graduate Seminar on "Social Welfare, Multiculturalism, and Democracy" in Dubrovnik, Croatia in April 2004 and then at the international conference "Genocide against Bosniaks of the UN Safe Area Srebrenica in July

primitiveness, and anti-Semitism prejudice. There may be negative attributes associated with Balkanism, but that negativity does not fall into the same category as racism, misogyny, and anti-Semitism. Balkanism is hardly guilty in the same way. Indeed, there may be something positive about Balkanism. It is not a pathology.

A second problem with this concluding sentence is that Todorova suggests an ambivalent relation between the Balkans and Europe. According to Todorova, while the Balkans stand parallel to Europe, they stand other to Europe at the same time. If anything, Europe uses the Balkans, not to know the Balkans, but to stipulate a knowledge of itself, that is, to define Europe. Edward W. Said calls this type of relation Orientalism: "European culture gained in strength and identity by setting itself off against the Orient as a sort of surrogate and even underground self" (1995, 3). Said then extends this point:

> I do not think that this idea can be overemphasized. Orientalism is premised upon exteriority, that is, on the fact that the Orientalist, poet or scholar, makes the Orient speak, describes the Orient, renders its mysteries plain for and to the West. He is never concerned with the Orient except as the first cause of what he says. (1995, 20–21)

Does Europe treat the Balkans "as a sort of surrogate and even underground self"? Are the Balkans exterior to Europe? Is there nothing intrinsically significant to the Balkans except to stand as "the first cause" for what is intrinsically significant to Europe?

These problems are significant, but there is an even more pressing problem in Todorova's final statement. Balkanism, Todorova says, cannot be grasped with dialectical thought. She indicates that the complementing and ennobling antiparticle, that is, the positive notion that counters the negative one that is Balkanism, has not yet been grasped. The Balkans are esoteric; their meaning exists beyond the grasp of dialectical inquiry. Although Todorova imagines a future when the complementing and ennobling antiparticle may be recognized and perhaps grasped, she indicates that such understanding does not yet exist. We are thus forced to ask, in the context of the Balkans, what does it take

---

1995: Lessons for the Future" in Srebrenica and Sarajevo, July 2005. Earlier versions were published as "Last Words / First Words" in *Odjek*.

to recognize the equivalent of the ennobling notions of antiracism, feminism, and the repudiation of anti-Semitism?

To turn the issue on its head, might Balkanism itself be a complementing and ennobling antiparticle to Europe, something interior as well as exterior, to what Europe is? Ironically enough, Todorova's concluding sentence puts the reader in a double-bind: the epistemology required for achieving what is proposed with the book's title is withheld. We cannot imagine the Balkans if their content is wholly negative in the identical way that racism, misogyny, and anti-Semitism are wholly negative. Nor can we imagine the Balkans if their content is just a stipulation, that is, a stipulation of what is other to Europe; nor can we imagine the Balkans if the subject is impervious to dialectical reasoning because its complementing and ennobling antiparticle remains forever concealed.

What is to be done? Let us retract, to some degree, the critique put forth. When responding negatively to negativity, the subject and object merge; no concept is developed. Let us instead recognize that there is something positive, indeed incisive, in Todorova's concluding sentence. If Europe is the soil upon which racism, misogyny, and anti-Semitism have flourished, what has flourished on the soil of the Balkans? What corresponding trope to racism, misogyny, and anti-Semitism grows on the soil of the Balkans? We must first recognize this subject before we can do the even more important work of grasping its complementing and ennobling antiparticle.

If racism, misogyny, and anti-Semitism are the regrettable progeny of Europe, what is the unwanted progeny of the Balkans? The thesis put forth and still stipulated at this point is that scapegoating flourishes on the soil of the Balkans much as racism, misogyny, and anti-Semitism are said to flourish on the soil of Europe. Racism, misogyny, anti-Semitism, and scapegoating, all four, of course, are related. They may even coincide in the same category. Scapegoating, however, is a distinct progeny; it is a child that vexes the cultural, social, and political history of the Balkans.

Scapegoating, of course, is biblical in its origins. A scapegoat is the sacrificial object, whether animal or human, through which a community seeks to purge itself of its sins. The transgressions of a community are projected onto the scapegoat. When the scapegoat is expelled or destroyed, so are the transgressions of the community which were symbolically but superficially projected onto the scapegoat.

Concretely, there is not a difference between being a victim and being a scapegoat. Both the victim and the scapegoat suffer. Analytically, there is a difference. Unlike the victim, whose suffering may be accidental or intentional, the scapegoat takes on symbolic significance. There is a ritual that constructs a demented understanding of the scapegoat. The result is prejudice and then violence under the cloak of blind righteousness. The person who is scapegoated loses his or her voice and comes to represent something arbitrarily connected to his or her self. The person is trapped in a ritual that has biblical nuances but inhuman consequences.

Scapegoating, of course, is not generic to the Balkans. There is not even a word in Serbo-Croatian that corresponds directly to the English word. Still, much as influenza from Europe spread all too easily among the susceptible native North American population, the pathology of scapegoating spreads all too easily among the inhabitants of the Balkans. The advantage of looking to the Balkans is not that scapegoating is absent elsewhere in the world, but that scapegoating occurs there in a clear and sophisticated manner.

First, let us reconsider a previously analyzed example. In *Yugoslavia: Death of a Nation*, Laura Silber and Allan Little write the following:

> Belgrade Television was firmly in Milošević's grip. It was the ideal tool for stirring up hatred against "the enemies of the Serbian people"—first Kosovo's Albanians, then the Slovenes, the Croats, and finally, the opposition in Serbia itself. (1996, 120)

How then did Slobodan Milošević come to power? Silber and Little note this incident at the beginning of his ascendancy: "The crowd roared, screaming for the arrest of the Albanian Party leader [Azem Vlasi]. Milošević answered: 'I can't hear you, but we will arrest those responsible including those who have used the workers. In the name of the socialist people of Serbia I promise this'" (1996, 68). Silber and Little then note that Dušan Mitević, chief of Belgrade TV and confidant of Milošević, said that this was Milošević at his best.

What is it about Milošević's utterance that is so admirable for Mitević? Milošević says he will arrest those who deceive the people, who are plotting against Yugoslavia, and who have used the workers. It is

Milošević, however, who, at this moment, is deceiving the people, plotting against Yugoslavia, and using the workers. The way in which Milošević describes Vlasi is less a description of Vlasi and more a description of himself. Milošević makes Vlasi his scapegoat. By transferring to Vlasi the crimes of which he himself is guilty, Milošević becomes something other than himself. Milošević's guilt in undermining the state of Yugoslavia is transferred to Vlasi, who was subsequently put on a show trial and imprisoned. At the same time, Milošević co-opts Vlasi's innocence; he assumes Vlasi's integrity.

During such events, the Serbian people identified with Milošević; that is, they identified with what Milošević was doing, namely, scapegoating. Milošević's unchecked use of the scapegoating ritual made his power seem unassailable, not only to people inside Serbia but also to those outside Serbia. While the subjects of the ritual changed, the ritual remained the same. First, Kosovar Albanians, then Croats, then Bosnian Muslims, and then the political opposition in Serbia were cast in the same light. Other Balkan leaders learned to copy the scapegoat ritual. That is, communities who were scapegoated retaliated by scapegoating the members of the community that had been scapegoating them.

Milošević even employed this technique while standing trial at the Hague. Milošević's line of defense was that he was the sacrificial goat for the period when NATO bombed Serbia and Kosovo in 1999. Leftists such as Michael Parenti and Harold Pinter, who publicly supported and defended Milošević, also employed this line of defense. The weapon that Milošević used to destroy communities in former-Yugoslavia he cynically used to defend himself at The Hague. He put himself in the place of the victims who he himself victimized and claimed victim status.

Consider the following comment regarding Milošević between Aleksa Djilas and Tom Butler.

> When our conversation turned to Milošević, Aleksa Djilas declaimed: "My position is unique in Belgrade: he's guilty, but don't extradite him!" He chuckled as he told me that Latinka Perović was "mad" at him for his stand. I asked what was wrong with handing such djubre ("trash") as Milošević over to the Hague. Here, the British educated Djilas shed his urbanity, spitting out his words in a manner that reminded me of his late father: "But that would make him into a scapegoat!" (Butler 2001)

Why oppose the need to arrest Milošević if he is guilty of war crimes, crimes against humanity, and genocide? On what basis does Djilas resist this imperative? Djilas suggests that Western leaders underestimate the power of scapegoating. He dreads its consequences because he witnessed how the scapegoating ritual was used in political discourse in Serbia so effectively. According to Djilas, the cost of not arresting Milošević remains less than the cost of arresting him: the consequences of scapegoating are too high for the Serbian nation to pay.

At a pragmatic level, events at the Hague seem to have proved Djilas right. Allowing Milošević to defend himself before the Tribunal without appropriate legal representation (Milošević is himself a lawyer) created a kind of media event at the trial. Before the Tribunal's judges, Milošević acted out a scapegoat role. Milošević constructed evidence for his case on the spot, as it were. Milošević's individual responsibility for the injustices that he inflicted on so many people and communities remained unrecognized even when directly witnessed. Before the Serbian people, Milošević became not only a scapegoat, but also a martyr, and the judicial process backfired. Milošević's untimely death before the completion of his trial confirms this reading.

While the concept of scapegoating has widely used descriptive power with respect to the discussion of evil, it is necessary to critique the limits of the concept as an explanation and expose the flaws inherent in the concept. The disciplines of psychology, sociology, theology, and rhetoric each have distinctive versions of the concept of scapegoating. It is worthwhile to distinguish these different versions and then collect their interconnectedness.

In psychology, the idea of scapegoating is used to explain victimization. As a scapegoat, an individual is treated as an object against whom the prejudice of the group is projected. The individual becomes a lightning rod for the group's hatred, which, in fact, is a self-hatred even though it is focused on another. Because the group, whether a family or a community, cannot live with this hatred of itself, it transfers the unwanted feeling to another. The transference occurs in a perverse manner in that the group's self-hatred is entrenched. Co-optation of the victim is necessary. Through the scapegoating dynamic, the group's self-hatred becomes self-perpetuating, which is why the ritual is both unhealthy and dysfunctional.

This pathology explains to a significant degree the grotesque acts of individuals and groups committing heinous crimes against Bosnian

Muslims and other Bosnians. At this point no more examples are needed.

In sociology, scapegoating is used to explain the way in which a community may attempt to establish order and tranquility. The scapegoat is an object lesson. In order for members of a society to feel secure, they ritualistically commit violence against one who has been singled out. Collectively, the members of the society inflict on one of its members what they all either consciously or unconsciously fear could be inflicted upon themselves. The group's collective anxiety triggers scapegoating, and the purpose is to relieve the group of its angst.

Although not a sociologist, René Girard is the most eloquent proponent of this theory. In *Violence and the Sacred*, Girard puts forth an eloquent account of scapegoating explicitly as a concept in literary criticism and implicitly as a sociological theory. Girard argues that scapegoating is necessary as well as inevitable in the history of a community. According to Girard, scapegoating is ritualized violence that, when done unanimously, effectively stops violence and establishes social harmony. If scapegoating is done unanimously with the consent of the entire community (the linchpin of his theorizing), it suppresses the possibility of reciprocity. "Unanimity is a formal requirement; the abstention of a single participant renders the sacrifice even worse than useless—it makes it dangerous" (1972, 100). The function of religion, Girard says, is to develop this sense of unanimity through symbolically ritualizing violence.

As a prelude to his formulation of scapegoating, Girard first articulates the state of nature that is called "the Hobbesian jungle":

> The fear generated by the kill-or-be-killed syndrome, the tendency to "anticipate" violence by lashing out first (akin to our contemporary concept of "preventive war") cannot be explained in purely psychological terms. . . . In a universe both deprived of any transcendental code of justice and exposed to violence, everyone has reason to fear the worst. The difference between a projection of one's own paranoia and an objective evaluation of circumstances has been worn away. (1972, 54)

Although Girard and Hobbes have an identical understanding of the state of nature as violent, lawless, and chaotic, Girard's solution with respect to the establishment of social order is antithetical to Hobbes's.

Therefore, to understand Girard's solution, it is best first to review Hobbes's.

What is the social contract? For Hobbes, the social contract represents the birth of society. Society is created when a collection of people recognizes that life becomes peaceful when they agree to suspend their use of force and fraud against each other and when this agreement is viewed as binding. Without a social contract, life among people is short, nasty, and brutish. Violence dominates. With a social contract, violence is viewed as unnecessary—necessarily unnecessary. This recognition lifts people out of the Hobbesian jungle, where interactions remained a matter of every man and woman for himself or herself and where every man and woman engaged in the limitless, albeit self-destructive, use of force and fraud. For Hobbes, society is nothing except a cognitive construction. Society is born when people collectively recognize the inherent rationality of the social contract. As rational beings, people recognize that the social contract is a more efficient means of attaining a peaceful and safe life than every individuals' unchecked use of force and fraud.

What convinces people to accept the social contract? For Hobbes the answer is strictly empirical. There is no moral principle here. The hellish experience of a war of all against all and our primal memory of this experience compels us to accept the rationality of the social contract. The history of social violence, then, is a record of forgetting and re-remembering this lesson, the ebb and flow of irrational and rational conduct. Society is the birth of the distinction between complying in deference to another's potential use of force or fraud and obeying out of respect for the authority and innate rationality of the social contract. Authority here is based on the notion that a group of people (a society) collectively accepts a rule as rationally binding.

Girard has a strikingly anti-Hobbesian understanding of social order. While Girard's theorizing depicts the presocial nature of human nature even more clearly than Hobbes, it shuns the foundational principles that the discipline of sociology inherits from Hobbes. Natural right is not suspended, nor is it critiqued. Natural right is instead masked behind a vulgar notion of social right. The notion that "might is right" is implicitly preserved through society's evolution. When society scapegoats unanimously, society becomes mighty and therefore rightful. For Girard, social right develops because it is the most forceful expression of natural right. For Girard, the primary foundation of society is its inherent lawlessness: we live in "a universe deprived of any transcendental code of justice" (1972, 54).

Girard says that violence is inevitable. Hobbes says that, thanks to the social contract, violence is not inevitable. It is true that in the state of nature violence is inevitable. It is necessary, however, to understand why violence is not inevitable in society. Girard and Hobbes each address the role of envy in recounting the origins of society. Envy, they say, is an intrinsic feature of the human species. Human beings are social; one way in which that sociability is expressed is through envy. For Girard, envy is always superior to rationality. Envy trumps rationality, which is why scapegoating rather than the social contract achieves social order. For Hobbes, rationality is superior to envy. If it were not, there would never be society. For Hobbes, rationality and envy, in fact, work together, collude together, to establish the social contract. The social contract is created not simply because of our rationality (the strict utilitarian understanding of social order) but also because of our capacity to put ourselves in the place of another. If we use violence against another, another will use violence against us. Envy, which puts oneself in the place of another, is turned into a positive rather than a negative force. Since we do not want violence to be brought to bear against ourselves, we do not want violence to be brought to bear against others. With rationality, envy is transformed into empathy. Without rationality, envy perpetuates violence.

It is therefore wrongheaded for Girard to argue that violence is imitable. Violence cannot truly be imitated. To imitate, we must put ourselves in the place of the other. Our conscience must link us to another. We imagine and anticipate what another feels. When there is this identification with the other, violence cannot occur.

Violence, of course, can be copied, and in the state of nature, violence is copied. Revenge copycats the violent deed of another. Copying occurs without identification. Copying is a natural behavior; it is not a social one because it lacks identification with another. To say that violence can be imitated is perverse and illogical; it places natural right, whether the natural right of a collective or the natural right of an individual, above social right. Social right is grounded in the trust that people imitate, that is, identify with, the rationality of the social contract.

For example, the Great Commandant, "Love thy neighbor as thyself," is a theological precept that makes violence inimitable. Likewise, the Golden Rule, "Do unto others as you would have them do unto you," is a normative principle that makes violence inimitable. The political commitment of Mohandas K. Gandhi to ahimsa as the love that brings about true social change makes violence inimitable. Gandhi knows that humans cannot inflict violence on another human being when they see that human being identifying with them and when they see that human being calling for them to identify with the one toward whom their violence is intended.

One reason that the concept of scapegoating is morally confusing is because multiple versions of the concept emerge simultaneously in scholarly discussions. While the different versions are neither independent nor mutually exclusive, their mixing can result in misunderstanding. In theology, there is also a concept of scapegoating, and this version lurks in the background of secular discussions of the phenomenon. It is important therefore to distinguish the version of scapegoating found in theology in order to separate it from the secular versions.

In the theology of the Abrahamic faiths, Christianity, Judaism, and Islam, God does not allow Abraham to sacrifice his son. God provides a ram as a substitute. The ram, not Abraham's son, is the scapegoat. The parable shows God's relation to humanity. God will not accept human sacrifices. Through Abraham, divine law becomes human law. In faithful communities, the scapegoating of human beings who are all created in God's image is taboo.

This imperative informs not just faithful communities but any community grounded in the principle of human rights. The dividing line between a barbaric society and a civilized society is the depth of a society's taboo against scapegoating. If the taboo is strong, there is social stability. Moral unanimity exists. If the taboo is feeble, there is anomie. Societies in which the political media and popular culture promote the scapegoating ritual unabashedly are barbaric, hardly societies at all. In such communities, the absence of a social contract is ignorantly perceived as the ideal social contract. Absolute freedom reigns with absolute terror. When societies use the scapegoating ritual to sustain social order and establish stability, human rights become nonexistent.

We have surveyed the concept of scapegoating in psychology, sociology, and theology. We have indicated how theology provides a counterversion to the concept of scapegoating found in psychology and sociology. In literature, there are stories that dramatize scapegoating. Interestingly, such stories are especially vivid in the literature of the

Balkans. Consider the Nobel Prize winner Ivo Andrić's (1977) *Bridge on the Drina*, in which there is at the beginning of the novel the gory impaling of Radosav. Andrić's latent nationalism is evident in the way that he frames and tells this tale. Radosav is a scapegoat in several senses within the novel. He is a scapegoat for the failure to complete the bequeathed bridge; he is an object-lesson to the citizens of Višegrad who observe this gruesome killing; and he is a martyr within the local Serbian community who idealize him as a Christ figure. This literary example of scapegoating is artful but morally confusing; it unclearly mixes the psychological, sociological, and theological aspects of the concept. Moreover, in every dramatic scene after this opening one, Andrić continues to employ the scapegoat structure to frame his narrative. The novel never develops from or transcends the scapegoating of Radosav, which remains the defining moment in the novel. In real life, this dramatization is dangerous; it is propaganda.

In the social sciences, scapegoating is a mechanism for expressing prejudice; in literary criticism, it is a symbolic mechanism for purging a community of dissonance and establishing solidarity within a seemingly functional community. Ironically, literary criticism's account is the more sociological. For the purging of the scapegoat to be functional, there must be identification as well as dis-identification. The scapegoat is not a stranger. The scapegoat comes from within the community. Radoslav was from Višegrad.

It is helpful now to consider the concept of scapegoating in the discipline of rhetoric because it helps synthesize the previously discussed concepts. Kenneth Burke provides a clear account of what scapegoating is for rhetoric with the notion of vicarious atonement.

> As such, [the scapegoat] is profoundly consubstantial with those who, looking upon it as a chosen vessel, would ritualistically cleanse themselves by loading the burden of their own iniquities upon it. Thus the scapegoat represents the principle of division in that its persecutors would alienate from themselves to it their own uncleanlinesses. For one must remember that a scapegoat cannot be "curative" except insofar as it represents the iniquities of those who would be cured by attacking it. In representing *their* iniquities, it performs the role of vicarious atonement (that is, unification, or merger, granted to those who have alienated their iniquities upon it, and so may be purified through its suffering). (1969, 406)

With the concept of vicarious atonement, Burke offers a critical understanding of scapegoating. To consider an example, what sort of vicarious atonement did the Serbian nation seek through Milošević's trial? Arresting Milošević in Belgrade and transferring him to the Hague divided Milošević from the Serbian people. Milošević represented the guilt of the Serbian people; in the name of a Greater Serbia Milošević initiated, planned, incited, and carried out genocide. The division that the Belgrade arrest created initiated a curative process. In offering up Milošević as a scapegoat, the Serbian nation gave some sort of reparation. The Serbian people cleansed themselves of their iniquities against their neighbors. The reparation, however, was unreal; as Burke says, it was vicarious, and this was Djilas's prophetic point.

Milošević is a metonym for the complicity of the Serbian people in genocide. After identification has been made, the scapegoat is reified. The community then expels its fetish. If the scapegoat has been identified with the transgressions of the community, it is necessary to cast out the scapegoat. The scapegoat has become a mirror in which the community sees its negative reflection. The mirror reflects the community's guilt. The community cannot tolerate seeing itself in the mirror; the identification is too painful because the identification is innate.

Another example of this point is the release of the infamous Scorpion video through the brave efforts of Nataša Kandić (Hemon 2005). The video films the military police from Serbia murdering six Bosnian men from Srebrenica in July 1995. It is like a home video, first showing Serb Orthodox priests blessing the men in the Scorpion militia before entering Bosnia. Later, the Scorpions are shown taking six men off a truck, forcing them to lie in a ditch and then march down a road to a field where they are shot with their hands tied behind their backs. After first shooting four of the men, the Serbian military police untie the hands of the two remaining men, who are ordered to carry the bodies into a house. After dragging the bodies through a field into a house, these two men, who were the least submissive in the group, are shot and left with the bodies of the others.

People living in Serbia and Bosnia-Herzegovina have viewed this video on television. Many Muslim families in Bosnia have copies of the tape in their homes. In a painstakingly slow manner, the video shows six men being taunted, degraded, mocked, brutalized, traumatized, and slaughtered. The Serbian militia laugh and snicker at their victims. The six men, one of whom is a sixteen-year-old boy, are objects against whom the anti-Muslim prejudice of the Serbian militia and anti-Bosnian ideology of Serbian nationalism are projected. These men become vessels for the antipathy that the murderers feel toward not only their victims but also themselves for participating in the mass killings around Srebrenica. The men's self-hatred is projected onto their victims, who they never touch except with their boots and rifles. The Serbian military police co-opt the last two men into their own victimization. The last two men are forced to carry the bodies of the men, who they watched being slowly shot, into an empty house before being killed themselves. The homoerotic features of the home video as it pans the backsides of the men are barely concealed; these homoerotic features are peppered among the machismo displays of power that pervade the video. It is like a snuff film but, unlike pornographic movies, in which a murder may be perfectly simulated, in this video murders occur and are filmed.

In the monograph *Genocide in Srebrenica, United Nations "Safe Area" in July 1995*, Smail Čekić, Muharem Kreso, and Bećir Macić write, "Srebrenica crystallized a truth understood only too late by the United Nations and the world at large: that Bosnia was as much a moral cause as a military conflict" (2001, 269). Bosnia is still a moral cause. One way to meet our responsibility to this truism is to seek answers to the question of why the mass killings in Srebrenica were allowed to occur. As stated in *Genocide in Srebrenica*, the fundamental but inadequately answered question is, "Why did the United Nations fail to deter the Serb attack on Srebrenica and the appalling events that followed when the United Nations had a mandate to deter the Serb attacks on Srebrenica" (Cekic, Kreso, and Macić 2001, 11)?

Through an application of the concept of scapegoating, it is possible to address the moral blindness and irresponsibility of the United Nations and the international community. Were the human beings in Srebrenica sacrificed for some goal based on global politics to which the victims themselves had no relation? Why did the United Nations not deter the attack against the safe area of Srebrenica despite its promise to defend the Srebrenica civilians, a promise that resulted in the Bosnian army surrendering the heavy weapons needed to protect the area? How did the Serbian general, Ratko Mladić, blackmail the French UN officer, Colonel Janvier, so effectively at their secret meetings? What explained the power that Mladić had over the United Nations after the Serbian army seized UN soldiers? Janvier's fear was that, in the hands of the Serbian army, UN soldiers would become scapegoats. This fear paralyzed and clouded Janvier's judgment. In order to rescue UN soldiers from this fate, the UN instead permitted thousands of civilians in Srebrenica to be substituted and mercilessly slaughtered in an utterly obscene and unconscionable manner. These civilians became scapegoats not only for Mladić and the Serbian army but also for the UN and the world at large. Mladić—with this tactical exchange—won the UN's complicity.

What was achieved on the part of Janvier through these deals with Mladić? Yes, he stopped Mladić from scapegoating UN soldiers by promising Mladić not to bomb the Serbian army in exchange for the release of the UN hostages. He, however, did not stop Mladić from scapegoating Bosnian civilians. The problem is the manner in which the UN stopped Mladić from scapegoating UN soldiers at the same time fueled Mladić's obscene use of the scapegoating ritual. The fact that Mladić could encompass the United Nations within his perverse ritual deepened his madness and inflamed his pathology.

One of the most morally egregious acts with respect to the UN failure to prevent mass killings in Srebrenica was the advice of Colonel Karremans, the commander of the Dutch forces stationed in the safe area, to the military and political leaders of Srebrencia. These leaders were told on the evening of July 10 that there would be massive NATO air strikes on the morning of July 11 to stop the advance of the Serbian army into Srebrenica. Karremans showed the Srebrenica leaders a map of areas around Srebrenica that would become a zone of death because NATO planes would destroy everything that moved in these areas. Karremans advised Bosnian soldiers defending Srebrenica to abandon their defense lines and stay clear of this area because NATO air strikes would occur the next morning. However, the NATO air strikes did not occur. The consequence of Karremans's advice was that the next day it was all too easy for the Serbian army to enter the town and commence with its genocide as the world watched.

When the Srebrenica leaders received this news from Karremans skeptically, Karremans is reported as having said, "Don't shoot the piano player" (Honig and Both 1996, 21–22; Rodhe 1997, 133). While authors writing on this exchange have noted that the Bosnian translator had trouble translating the metaphor, the terminology is cryptic even for English speakers. Was Karremans the piano player playing an out-of-tune piano? Was Karremans providing music, a welcomed message, which should be enjoyed rather than killed? At this moment, evil was fully present.

While it may be impossible to provide an historically adequate account as to why this act of bad faith took place between Karremans and the Srebrenica leaders in this way and in this manner, it is possible to provide a meaningful account of the consequences of this exchange. Through this advice from Karremans, the UN tied the hands of the victims in Srebrenica for their grotesque slaughter by the Serbian army. The UN enabled the Serbian genocide because the UN itself was entrapped in the scapegoat ritual and did not know how either to escape or to stop the ritual.

It is in the interest of the UN and everyone to learn from this horrible mistake. The task now is to construct the completing and ennobling antiparticle to scapegoating, the repudiation of scapegoating, its antidote, and demonstrate how it grows in the Balkans, as well as the antidotes to racism, misogyny, and anti-Semitism that grow in Europe. The writing of Émile Durkheim, in contrast to Hobbes, suggests that the notion of social right is grounded in something more than empirical experience. In his essay on the Dreyfus affair, "Individualism and the Intellectuals," which itself is a sociological critique of the scapegoating ritual in France, Durkheim writes, "And since each of us incarnates something of humanity, each individual consciousness contains something divine and thus finds itself marked with a character which renders it sacred and inviolable to others" (1973, 52). Since each individual is sacred and thus inviolable, scapegoating is taboo, necessarily taboo. Since each individual is inviolable, no individual and no community can accept the scapegoating of any individual. When one is persuaded by this principle, one recognizes that there is moral unity only when the state itself defends this conviction. Scapegoating can never become unanimous because no individual would ever consent to being scapegoated and the person scapegoated must be selected from the community. Girard's theorizing is based on an irrational fiction. What is, in fact, unanimous is the taboo against scapegoating, and this unanimity is metaphysical as well as empirical.

Durkheim demonstrates how the problem of social order cannot be resolved without reference to human rights. Sociologists borrow from the transcendental language of human rights even if they do so without acknowledging their indebtedness to this language. According to Durkheim, the social contract equally serves the interests of the individual and society: "Not only is individualism distinct from anarchy; but is henceforth the only system of beliefs which can ensure the moral unity of the country" (1973, 50). How is it that individualism and the moral unity of the country are affirmed simultaneously? Durkheim argues that a state may never accept scapegoating as a way to establish order because "there is no reason of State which can excuse an outrage against the person when the rights of the person are placed above the State" (46). Durkheim observes that when society "tolerates acts of sacrilege it abdicates any sway over men's minds" (53). The transgression of this principle of governance explains the spiral of violence in not only former-Yugoslavia, but also in Israel's oppression of Palestinians and the U.S. military occupation of Iraq.

Consider Robert Hayden's critical discussion of the Dayton Accord in "Focus: Constitutionalism and Nationalism in the Balkans":

> The Dayton Constitution . . . gives priority to human rights. Yet these are meaningless. As James Madison notes in 1787, "In framing a government . . . the great difficulty lies in this: you must first enable the government to control the governed; and in the next place oblige it to control itself." (1995, 68)

Hayden's citation to Madison is telltale. How does a government control the governed? One way in which the government controls the governed is through the use of force and fraud. Madison, however, indicates that if all the government does is control the governed, no matter how efficiently and effectively, it is not a government. Such a government can only resort to increasingly sophisticated forms of force and fraud, and this, we see, is the road to hell. The government itself is out of control.

Madison says that the government is obliged to control itself. But what obliges a government to control itself? There is only one way to oblige a government to control itself: when it gives priority to human rights. Giving priority to human rights is tantamount to the government controlling itself. The commitment to human rights obliges a government to control itself as it controls the governed. The commitment to human rights wins the consent of the governed to be governed, to be controlled, by the government. The best, the most efficient, and so, ultimately, the most rational way for a government to control the governed is for the government to respect human rights because respecting human rights wins the consent of the governed to be controlled by what controls the government.

11. Theorizing Evil with Socratic Naiveté

But is evil then not, by its nature, an action? Not at all; action is only the type of evil happening which makes evil manifest. *But does not evil action stem precisely from a decision to evil?* The ultimate meaning of our exposition is that it too stems primarily from indecision, providing that by decision we understand, not a partial, a psuedo decision, but that of the whole soul (emphasis added).

—Martin Buber

Evil is difficult to comprehend theoretically. Socrates avoided this task, and it is important to understand why. When someone knows that an act is wrong (truly knows that it is wrong), someone will not willingly commit the act. Doing wrong, according to Socrates, is a matter of ignorance and nothing else.

Socrates' refusal to theorize evil exasperated his interlocutors. In Plato's *Gorgias*, Polus asked why Socrates argued as if he were unaware of evil. "But can they not kill whoever they please, like dictators, and inflict confiscation and banishment on anyone they choose?" Socrates replied that, while tyrants do these terrible things, they are "the least powerful persons in a state. They do practically nothing that they will, only what they think best." Polus replied, "Well, isn't that to enjoy

---

Portions of this chapter were previously published as "Civilno društvo na Balkanu" and "Socratic Medicine for Radovan Karadžić" in *Odjek*.

great power?" Socrates answered no and asked, "Do you think it a benefit when a man devoid of wisdom does what seems best to him?" Polus still objected, and Socrates became empathetic, "They don't do what they really will. Prove me wrong" (Plato 1960, 48–50).

At the beginning of *Nicomachean Ethics*, Aristotle states the principle that sustains Socrates' refusal to theorize evil: "Every art and every inquiry, and similarly every action and pursuit, is thought to aim at some good; and for this reason the good has been rightly declared to be that at which all things aim" (quoted in Blum 1978, 1). In order for action to be action, it must aim at some good. If evil is action, toward what end does it aim? Can evil aim at some good and still be evil? To be evil, evil must aim at what is not good. Once evil becomes action, once it aims toward some good, it is no longer evil. For Socrates, the unbreakable character of this logic exonerates him from accounting for evil. From the perspective of thought itself, evil does not exist. For Socrates, it is not a serious subject.

If, however, we could report to Socrates the violence inflicted upon people and the communities of Bosnia-Herzegovina, would Socrates say that Ratko Mladić and Radovan Karadžić, the individuals responsible for planning, initiating, leading, and sustaining these crimes, did not "do what they willed"? Would Socrates say that Mladić and Karadžić had "the least power" in the cities of Bosnia-Herzegovina during the war?

It is worth citing *Gorgias* at length:

Socrates: Then when we walk we walk as a means to the good, because we think it the better course; and when we stand still on the other hand we stand still from the same motive as a means to the good. Do you agree?
Polus: Yes.
Socrates: And when we kill or banish or confiscate, if we ever do so, we act from a belief that it is better for us to do so than not?
Polus: Certainly.
Socrates: Then men do all these things as a means to the good?
Polus: Yes.
Socrates: We agreed, didn't we, that we do not will acts that are means, but the ends to which they are means?

Polus: Of course.

Socrates: So we do not will a man's death or banishment or loss of property simply for its own sake; we will it if it brings advantage, but not if it brings the reverse. As you say yourself, we will what is good; we do not will what is indifferent, still less what is bad. Am I right, Polus, or not? Why don't you answer?

Polus: You are right.

Socrates: Then, if that is granted, when a dictator or an orator kills or banishes or confiscates because he believes it to be to his advantage, and it turns out to be to his disadvantage, we must allow that he does what he pleases, mustn't we?

Polus: Yes.

Socrates: But does he do what he wills, when what he does turns out to be bad? Why don't you answer?

Polus: I agree that he doesn't do what he wills.

(Plato 1960, 51–52)

Polus begrudgingly agrees with Socrates. Nobody wills to kill or banish people from cities as an end-in-itself when these things are in fact not good.

When Mladić and Karadžić walk, they walk because they think that it is good. When they stand still, they stand still because they think that it is good. As actors, Mladić and Karadžić pursue good things rather than evil things. Consider this report from Adil Zulfikarpašić on Karadžić at a joint meeting in Zvornik with the Muslim Bosniak Organization and the SDS in 1991:

> That meeting was very important for the fact that the main representative of the Serbs, Karadžić, said that Greater Serbia was a wonderful dream but could not be achieved in Bosnia, that the Serbs should know that, and that real life differed from such dreams. He then said quite reasonably that in those parts of Bosnia where Serbs and Bosniaks lived together, in half of the municipalities the Bosniaks were the majority, and in the other half the Serbs, so that where the Serbs had the majority they should protect the Muslims, and where the Muslims had the majority they should protect the Serbs. The only prospect for the future lay in

living together. Even today, when visitors to the Bosniak Institute watch our video recording of that meeting they say it is astonishing the degree to which the Serbs had actually accepted the agreement and renounced the idea of Greater Serbia. (1998, 181)

Karadžić knew that what he thought best, the dream of a Greater Serbia, was not what he willed. When Karadžić said before the war in Zvornik, "The only prospect for the future lay in living together," he was intelligent. Karadžić knew what was good. How many lives would have been saved and how much destruction would have been avoided if Karadžić had acted according to what he willed?

The mass murders in Srebrenica and uncountable other places throughout Bosnia-Herzegovina were not good. The conscience of the world knows this as a matter of direct acquaintance for which no rational proof is required. Even the superego of Karadžić knows this as a matter of direct acquaintance for which no rational proof is required.

After hearing of Karadžić's crimes against humanity, Socrates would say, "Do you think it is a good if someone does whatever seems best to him when he has no intelligence?" Hannah Arendt would support this position. With the concept of the banality of evil, Arendt shows solidarity with Socrates' refusal to theorize evil.

> It is indeed my opinion now that evil is never "radical," that it is only extreme, and that it possesses neither depth nor any demonic dimension. It can overgrow and lay waste the whole world precisely because it spreads like a fungus on the surface. It is "thought-defying," as I said, because thought tries to reach some depth, to go to the roots, and the moment it concerns itself with evil, it is frustrated because there is nothing. That is its "banality." Only the good has depth and can be radical. (correspondence cited in Bernstein 1996, 138–39)

To have depth, one seeks some good. To be radical, one seeks some good. Evil is "thought-defying" because it does not seek some good.

During the war, many journalists interviewed Karadžić. The question that journalists would ask in one way or another was what was his motivation. What reasoning guided his conduct? Karadžić would say that he was doing what he thought best, say, for "his people" or a "Greater Serbia." This response was banality: while Karadžić was perhaps doing what he thought best, he was not doing what he willed. He knew that "in those parts of Bosnia where Serbs and Bosniaks lived together, in half of the municipalities the Bosniaks were the majority, and in the other half the Serbs, so that where the Serbs had the majority they should protect the Muslims, and where the Muslims had the majority they should protect the Serbs" (Karadžić quoted in Zulfikarpašić 1998, 181). Karadžić, however, acted contrary to what he knew.

Pundits and journalists, however, favored the contrasting position; they favored the notion that Karadžić was doing what he wanted, that Karadžić wanted to inflict mass murder and genocide upon the people and society of Bosnia-Herzegovina. Thomas Cushman, for example, writes, "At base, evil is *action*" (2000, 33). Understanding Karadžić as deep rather than as banal was a better story line; understanding Karadžić as a radical nationalist rather than as a shallow politician was better news. If Karadžić were deep and radical, who could stop such a powerful man? In contrast, if Karadžić were banal and superficial, not doing what he wanted because he did not at all know what he wanted, who could fail to stop him if they would but try?

Whenever human thought seeks to grasp evil as anything more than banal, the Socratic figure haunts the discussion. Consider the following passage in *Literature and Evil* from Georges Bataille, "We explore Evil in as far as we think it Good, and, inevitably, the exploration is doomed to failure and ridicule. But this does not make it any the less interesting" (1973, 149). Socrates' objection is embedded in Bataille's statement. "We explore Evil in as far as we think it Good" (1973, 149). For Bataille, Socrates' objection, however, does not hold; that is, it does not stop Bataille from conducting his inquiry even though he knows that it is doomed to failure and ridicule. For Bataille, the exploration remains interesting. How, though, is what is thought-defying interesting?

We now see the modern retort to Socrates' refusal to theorize evil; postmodernism says that evil is oriented. Jeffery C. Alexander writes, "social evil can be and often is sought as an end in itself" (2001, 170). To resolve the contradiction of this polemic, we could say that evil represents the good of not aspiring toward the good. For evil, the way to seek good is not to seek good, and this aim becomes an end-in-itself. Once evil, however, aims at some good, even the good of not aiming toward the good, evil is no longer evil. Evil loses itself with the will to seek good, albeit in a contradictory way. Evil becomes nonevil, thoughtless.

If there were truly an ontology for evil, the integrity of action would disintegrate. Consider Slavoj Žižek when he implicitly attempts to formulate evil as an end-in-itself.

> Is there a specific kind of knowledge which renders impossible the act, a knowledge which can no longer be co-opted by cynical distance (I know what I am doing, but I am nevertheless doing it.)? (1996, 512)

To reframe Žižek's question, can I know that I am doing evil and nevertheless do evil? Is there a specific kind of knowledge, namely evil, that renders impossible the act? Is it possible to act without seeking some good? Žižek seeks to develop an account of evil as oriented, but he is unable to do so.

Consider again the incisive accounts of Karadžić by Semezdin Mehmedinović. Mehmedinović recalls a conversation he had with Karadžić in Sarajevo before the war:

> We were in the Writer's Club one summer afternoon and he was telling me, with great enthusiasm, about a movie he had seen the day before. The movie was *Sophie's Choice*, and Radovan, speaking from the professional perspective of someone concerned with the human psyche, interpreted in great detail the various aspects of Meryl Streep's spiritual state in the scene where a German officer presents her with the following choice: which of her two children should be saved, since one would have to be killed. Underground, my hair stood on end as I remembered his rational analysis of Sophie's choice. (1998, 19)

Is Karadžić a person fascinated by evil? If he is a person fascinated with evil, at what point did he turn? Did Karadžić will evil rather than good? Mehmedinović notes, "The ghastly scene from *Sophie's Choice* was endlessly repeated in Bosnia: Karadžić's soldiers put mothers in the same position in which Meryl Streep found herself in the cinematic reconstruction of events that took place in a German concentration camp" (1998, 20).

Is radical evil possible? Can a human being do evil knowing that it is evil? Is Karadžić an evil person or a person who does not know what he wants? How this question is answered influences the decisions of the international elite on whether, when, and how to apprehend Karadžić.

If he is seen as evil, it may seem futile and vain to arrest him. If Karadžić is evil, he is incorrigible. What is the point of arresting him? It would change nothing; it could never undo what he did. The task can wait until he dies, when, of course, it would be pointless.

If Socrates were to meet Karadžić, what mirror would Socrates hold up to Karadžić to look into? Would Karadžić see himself? The approach that Socrates would undertake (as he did with Thrasymachus in "Book One" of *The Republic*) would be to persuade Karadžić that, even if he were doing what he thought best when he committed war crimes, crimes against humanity, and genocide, he was never doing what he wanted. Socrates would assume that once Karadžić became thoughtful, he would agree that the sociocide referred to euphemistically as ethnic cleansing was not action insofar as action must pursue some good. The mindless murders, immense destruction, unconscionable bad faith, and unthinkable injustices that Karadžić inflicted upon people in Bosnia-Herzegovina exemplified an absence of intelligence.

Would Karadžić eventually blush in such a conversation? Would Karadžić exemplify an *individual* consciousness? In Plato's *The Republic,* toward the end of the conversation between Socrates and Thrasymachus, we read the following:

> Now, Thrasymachus did not agree to all of this so easily as I tell it now, but he dragged his feet and resisted, and he produced a wonderful quantity of sweat, for it was summer. And then I saw what I had not yet seen before—Thrasymachus blushing. (1968, 29)

Why does Thrasymachus, once he sees that he is refuted, blush? Why does he not, like Anytus in *Meno*, get angry, threaten Socrates, and walk away? Why does he not, like Callicles in *Gorgias*, stubbornly refuse to answer any more questions? Jacob Klein remarks, "What is being said in a Platonic dialogue must be watched most carefully: every word counts; some casually spoken words may be more important than lengthy, elaborate statements" (1977, 2). This statement from Klein recommends treating the seemingly superficial exchanges between Socrates and Thrasymachus as a crucial aspect of the dialogue, equal to if not greater in importance to the philosophical argument itself.

Thrasymachus's blush is an expression of his experience upon being refuted. While involuntary, the blush comes from within Thrasymachus; it reveals him. It reveals his soul. Thrasymachus's blush exemplifies his awareness of the contradiction between what he had been arguing for, namely, that the unjust are not only stronger but also better than the just, and what he knows, namely, that the just are not only better but also stronger than the unjust.

Thrasymachus's blush surprises Socrates, who sees for the first time what Emmanuel Levinas would call Thrasymachus's face. It is an encounter. Levinas says, "The face before me summons me, calls for me, begs for me, as if the invisible death, that must be faced by the Other, pure otherness, separated, in some way, from any whole, were my business" (1989, 83). Thrasymachus's blush reveals his face. The blush is a demand, not a question. The blush requires Socrates to continue discussing justice for another nine books. Short dialogues are no longer sufficient. Given the responsibility that Thrasymachus's blush puts upon him, Socrates assumes a duty toward not only Thrasymachus, but also Glaucon and Adeimantus, who seek to carry on Thrasymachus's argument.

Will Karadžić blush? Many in Bosnia after suffering Karadžić's heinous crimes would say that Karadžić is incapable of blushing. Karadžić's followers, moreover, do not want their leader to be arrested and taken to the Hague because if he were to be taken there and if he were to blush, it would mean that Karadžić was not an evil man. It would mean that during the war Karadžić only did what he thought best but never did what he willed. It would mean that Karadžić did what he did with no intelligence.

If Karadžić is indeed incapable of blushing either at the Hague or anyplace else, then his crimes against humanity have so permanently damaged his soul that he is incapable of suffering a refutation. This does not mean that he is evil, at least according to Socrates. It means that he is incorrigible, no longer subject to reason and his innate desire for good. His conscience remains permanently asleep to avoid the nightmare of waking up. A Manichean lullaby, sung by followers, keeps his conscience asleep. The key lyric in this lullaby is the notion of radical evil.

If Karadžić were in fact to blush, it would put a demand upon the international community. Perhaps the international community wants to keep Karadžić hidden. Consider the "wanted posters" that dot the government buildings and public places of Bosnia-Herzegovina offering large sums of money for information leading to Karadžić's arrest. On the posters, we see the face of Karadžić, the face of someone who never saw the face of Bosnians. Levinas says, "The first word of the face is the 'Thou shalt not kill.' It is an order. There is a commandment in the appearance of the face, as if a master spoke to me" (1989, 83). Why display Karadžić's face so brazenly? If we see another's face, we cannot kill the other. Karadžić never saw the faces of others. Why should Karadžić's victims now have to see his face excruciatingly displayed in public places? The denotative meaning of these "wanted posters" (after the war there is now the rule of law) belies the connotative meaning of the "wanted posters" (there is still no respect for human dignity or justice).

The international community was waiting for Slobodan Milošević to blush at the Hague. The potential justice of the trial was that, at some point, Milošević would blush, however involuntarily, and the world would witness this blush. Imagine Milošević blushing on the witness stand at some critical moment and saying not only to his victims but also to his followers, "I was wrong. I am terribly sorry." The followers of Milošević prayed that Milošević would never blush, that he would never suffer a refutation, an authentic conviction. If Milošević were to blush, his followers would have to follow suit.

Milošević's untimely death before his trial at the Hague was completed is a tragedy. The trial lasted too long. Witnessing Milošević blush would have restored the rule of law and ensured social stability in Bosnia as well as Serbia. Such an event would have been immeasurably priceless. Nothing else could have brought peace and established justice in Bosnia so easily.

Consider now another likely and horrific ending to this history. What happens if Karadžić dies of natural causes without being brought to justice? What if he is never arrested? Will the Serbian Orthodox Church bury him? Where? Will the Serbian Orthodox Church bury Karadžić in Montenegro where his mother lived? In Serbia, near Belgrade? In Bosnia-Herzegovina? In Pale? Will Karadžić be buried next to one of the mass grave sites for which he is responsible? Near Srebrenica? Will the Serbian Orthodox Church bury Karadžić in several places repeatedly throughout Republika Srpska as it did Prince Lazar?

In 1991, Orthodox Serbs throughout former-Yugoslavia gathered to view Prince Lazar's remains. The bones of this legendary Serbian hero were passed around monasteries in former-Yugoslavia, places that were simultaneously claimed as Serbian lands. This event as much as anything triggered the pathos of ethnic tension. Displaying the remains of Lazar through Yugoslavia with repeated burials evoked and transfigured the ethical spirit of many, although not all, Serbian families. Through this public ritual Serbian families came to see their ethical spirit as grounded exclusively in their Serbian ethnicity. They became disconnected to their Yugoslav citizenship. What Hegel (1977, 464–82) calls the divine law of the human spirit became the dominating ethical spirit, which fomented nationalism and fueled the subsequent evil. Family and state became indistinguishable. In identifying exclusively with the ethical spirit that Hegel formulates as divine law, Serbian communities forgot their ethical spirit as modern citizens of Yugoslavia. They became blind to the complementary ethical spirit that Hegel formulates as human law. Human law, Hegel says, represents the rights of citizens and the moral authority of the state. Justice, Hegel says, is the substance of human law. Nationalism, whether Serbian, Croatian, Bosniak, or Albanian, displaces human law with divine law. Nationalism disfigures the ethical orientations of a society.

Civil society is a bridge. Civil society is a bridge between two distinct parts of society. Civil society links the family and the state, the private realm and the public domain. It is the bridge where people interact in the public domain, do commerce, maintain schools, secure marriage licenses, affirm culture, and so on. It is not a bridge between two different ethnic groups. Nationalism damages civil society.

In 2000, five years after the war in Bosnia, the reburial of the nationalistic Serbian poet, Jovan Dučić, in Trebinje, a part of Bosnia in Republika Srpska, replicates the political character and ethical pathos of the reburial of Prince Lazar in 1991. Both burials were sponsored by the Serbian Orthodox Church. The Serbian President Vojislav Koštunica attended this reburial in Bosnia-Herzegovina before ever having visited the capital of Bosnia-Herzegovina as Serbia's head of state. Koštunica agreed to visit Sarajevo and meet with officials at the city's airport only after intense pressure from the international community. As the Serbian President, Koštunica is obliged to acknowledge human law before divine law, which is not to deny his right to a particular relation to divine law. It is, though, to deny his right to privilege divine law, the divine law of family customs, over and above human law, the human law of the state. It is to deny his right as a nationalist to make family and state indistinguishable not only for himself but also for the citizens in his state.

Civil society has two important functions. It keeps the family and the state connected, and it keeps the family and the state independent. It is unhealthy for the family to be self-sufficient. The life of the family digresses and becomes tribal. It is also unhealthy for the state to assume sole responsibility for civil society. The life of the state becomes totalitarian. To be a strong bridge between the family and the state, civil society needs to be both fair and just. The family expects fairness from civil society, and fairness is represented with the good of cooperation grounded in a principle of equity. The state expects justice from civil society, and justice is represented with practices guided by truth and reason. Nationalism is dysfunctional because it makes civil society and the state one entity, and the family loses its independence.

These events sponsored by the Serbian Orthodox Church involving the remains of Prince Lazar and then Jovan Dučić usurp the ethical spirit of society. As we learn from reading the Greek tragedy, *Antigone*, the burial ritual is the one and only time that the ethical spirit of the family rightfully takes precedence over the ethical spirit of the state. Despite the harsh edicts of King Creon, Antigone must bury her dead brother. It is her duty. Nationalism, however, is an unhealthy collective sentiment because it seeks to suspend the dominion of human law, not only during the time of the burial ritual, but also during all times. Nationalism uses divine law to displace human law permanently. In doing so, nationalism destroys not only the state but also the family.

It will be a nightmare if Karadžić dies without being punished. It will be a nightmare if Karadžić is buried by the Serbian Orthodox Church in the noble land of Bosnia without first being punished. By avoiding the problem of apprehending Karadžić today, the international community creates an even more intractable problem tomorrow. When Karadžić dies, the Serbian Orthodox Church will be in control of the situation; it will use divine law to continue to exercise dominion over the state. To fail to arrest Karadžić today perpetuates a fatalism to which not only nationalist Serbs but also the international community have become fixated. The toxicity of this fatalism spreads to other regions of the world, and the situation paralyzes the future of people in Bosnia. If Karadžić is buried in Bosnia without being arrested for doing so much to destroy this country, peace will seem impossible and war inevitable.

If convicted at the Hague, as part of his punishment, Karadžić should be taken to mass grave sites throughout Bosnia and told to apologize to his victims and their families, and these apologies should be broadcast on Belgrade Television and throughout the world. It will be better not only morally but also pragmatically to apprehend Karadžić now and put him in a situation where there is the greatest opportunity for him to blush and for the world to witness it.

12. Sociocide: A New Paradigm for Evil

> I have indicated my skepticism about the very idea of a *theory* of evil, if this is understood as a complete account of what evil *is*. I do not think that such a theory is possible, because we cannot anticipate what new forms of evil or vicissitudes of evil will appear.
>
> —Richard Bernstein

During the war in Bosnia, home after home was burned. Gunners methodically shelled from the hills house after house along streets in villages, towns, and cities. Traveling through the countryside of Bosnia after the war, one still sees how immense this devastation is. Burned-out frames of homes dot the hills. Empty shells of houses are found in every locale.

Why was the violence brought to bear in this particular way against the people of Bosnia? Consider the significance of the home as recounted by the cultural anthropologist, Tone Bringa:

> It often took ten to twenty years to finish a modern house. Only when we realize the amount and length of the hard work and effort which families have invested in the building of their house (and home), can we fully understand the tragedy of the systematic

---

Portions of the chapter were presented as "Reflections on War as Sociocide" at the Croatian Sociological Association Meeting, December 2002, Zagreb, Croatia.

burning of homes in rural Bosnia in the war and the devastating effect it has on people. When they lose their house, they lose all they have worked for in the past and much of what they would have lived for in the future. Particularly for the man as husband and father, the house he managed to build symbolized his social worth; it was proof of his hard work and commitment to his family and their future well-being. But the house or *kuća* also represented the moral unity of the household and the moral quality of its members, and while men were the builders of the house, women were the guardians of its moral values. (1995, 85–86)

What did it mean to wantonly destroy so many homes? Armed conflicts have taken on a twisted orientation. Not only in Bosnia but also in Rwanda, Chechnya, the Middle East, and now Iraq armed conflict assumes a demented purpose. Not only are houses destroyed, but also the prestige of the home. Not only are women and children murdered, but also the city itself, its rituals and ways of life. Not only are a particular group of people and its infrastructures assaulted, but also its history and collective memory. Not only is a social system demolished, but also society itself. In the first case, the violence is called domicide; in the second, urbicide; and in the third, genocide. In the fourth case, however, it is necessary to introduce a new term, a neologism, sociocide.

What then is sociocide? Sociocide is an inadequately theorized concept. It is not possible to understand evil as action because, as Aristotle (1962) states, action must aim at some good. It, though, is possible to understand the consequences of evil. We cannot directly witness evil because it is empty. We can, though, directly witness the result of evil. The ultimate result of evil is sociocide, whether at the individual or collective level.

The questions to address are What is it to kill society?, Is it possible to kill society?, and What would the murdering of a society mean? Consider Immanuel Kant's idealistic understanding of states at war in *Perpetual Peace*, "No state shall, during war, permit such acts of hostility which would make mutual confidence in the subsequent peace impossible" (1917, 114). With this statement, Kant imagines that during war a state is farsighted enough to think about its future relation with its enemy and ethical enough to ensure the possibility of mutual confidence in the subsequent peace.

Bosnia's enemies conducted war in the exact opposite way. Milošević's Belgrade regime not only permitted but also planned acts of hostility whose purpose was to render trust and mutual confidence in the subsequent peace impossible. Such was the guiding principle with which violence was brought to bear against the people and communities of Bosnia. War was conducted to utterly destroy one state's relation to another.

It helps to consider the argument inverted. Hegel provides an opposing point of view of the objective consequences of war; he formulates a positive relation between war and its impact on society:

> In order not to let them [families and private communities] get rooted and settled in this isolation and thus break up the whole into fragments and let the common spirit evaporate, government has from time to time to shake them to the very centre by War. By this means it confounds the order that has been established and arranged, and violates their right to independence, while the individuals (who, being absorbed therein, get adrift from the whole, striving after inviolable self-existence [*Fürsichseyn*] and personal security), are made, by the task thus imposed on them by government, to feel the power of their lord and master, death. By thus breaking up the form of fixed stability, spirit guards the ethical order from sinking into merely natural existence. (1977, 474)

Hegel argues that the social function of war is to reestablish a society's solidarity. This function is not just a consequence of war, but also a cause of war. In *Habits of the Heart,* Americans are depicted as increasingly private and self-centered, lacking a sense of civic commitment and social responsibility. The authors of *Habits of the Heart* call this quality ontological individualism (Bellah et al. 1985, 143). Hegel argues that, when society is in such an anomic state, war is necessary in order to confound the fragmentation of the society and reassert the state's significance. War positively establishes that solidarity required for a society to function. When families and private communities strive exclusively after their inviolable self-existence and absolute personal security, society is threatened. According to Hegel, war shatters and repairs this negative development.

In the context of Bosnia, war served the opposite function. The purpose and the manner in which war was conducted was to destroy society. Recall what was stated earlier. From 1992 to 1995, approximately one-quarter of a million or more people were killed; one-quarter of a million were maimed or injured; one-quarter of a million were held in concentration camps; and 2.5 million, more than half the population, were driven from their homes. Before the war, Bosnia had 4.5 million inhabitants. How are we to understand the magnitude of this interpersonal violence within a society? At some point, does the society in and of itself cease to exist?

Ozren Žunec, a sociologist in Croatia, studies the impact of war on society.

> All wars have effects on societies. The most destructive are armed conflicts which, in addition to social loses, leave societal losses, that is, the kind of devastation of society which imperils its very survival. "Societal" . . . is a theoretical concept and relates to society as a system that enables, organizes, and gives meaning to empirical society. (1999, 96)

Previous chapters have pointed out the severe "societal" losses during the war in Bosnia. Whether addressing the latent function of ethnic cleansing, the transgression of the burial funeral, the degradation ceremony, the crime of rape, the betrayal of intellectual figures, the disfigurement of language, or the scapegoat ritual, societal losses were heavy.

James Gow states that over the course of a decade, "the committing of war crimes was the essence of Serbian strategy" (2003, 2). Gow argues, "Ethnic cleansing was not a contingent phenomenon of a primitive, or bestial, culture, but a strategy involving rational calculations and decisions on the creation and use of means to achieve the ends" (2003, 306). He recounts these horrendous war crimes, addressing from an empirical point of view the questions of who, where, why, how, and what, and interweaving the answers to these questions into an informative testimony. This approach is to depict the crimes against humanity of the Serbian project as an oriented course of action, an example of the continuation of politics by "other means." For Gow, action is the unit of analysis, and in the social sciences action is composed of five analytical elements: (1) an actor or actors, (2) a context or set of conditions, (3) a purpose, (4) a means or instrument, and (5) a normative orientation, whether morally or culturally constructed, upon which action, in this case the action of war, negatively or positively draws. For each of these elements, Gow reviews the relevant findings and surveys the significant examples, of which there are many; he then formulates the interdependence of these five elements of the action frame of reference in relation to each other. As a political institution committed to a "Serbian project," the Belgrade regime brought unconscionable violence to bear against the people, heritage, tradition, and communities of its neighbors.

Talcott Parsons, the sociologist who best articulated the centrality of the action frame of reference to the social sciences, was fond of citing Alfred Marshall, who said, "The most reckless and treacherous of all theorists is he who professes to let facts and figures speak for themselves" (1968, 10 n.1). Gow's descriptions of events are shrewd and fluent; his analysis is credible and encompassing. Gow's accounts are so incontestable that there is no room for doubt with respect to his thesis, "A strategy of war crimes defines the war" (2003, 30). Still, at a moral level, there is something unsatisfactory with this analysis. Gow inflates the rationality of war criminals like Slobodan Milošević and Ratko Mladić and exaggerates the utilitarian efficiency of their criminality. This inflation gives an illusion of credibility and sanity to the madness of these horrendous events.

According to ancient philosophers, in order for action (in this case, the action of war) to be action, it must aim toward some good. If a deed cannot be conceived of as aiming toward some good, the deed cannot be conceived of as action. If the war crimes in Brčko, Foča, Sarajevo, Srebrenica, Zvornik, and uncountable other places in Bosnia-Herzegovina, were actions, toward what good did they aim? No utilitarian calculus can interpret these deeds as aiming toward some good. Metaphysically, it is a mistake to treat these crimes against humanity as anything except banal. To do more, to inflate the rationality of the events as if the actors were seeking some good, is to be co-opted by evil.

Sonja Biserko (2005), Norman Cigar (1995), Michael Sells (1996), Mirko Djordjević (1996), Sabrina Ramet (1996), and Radmila Radić (2000) have all critically described the leading role of the Serbian Orthodox Church in the incitement of the Serbian people to turn against their neighbors and fellow citizens:

> With Milošević's arrival in power, the Serb Orthodox Church was returned to public prominence in order to facilitate implementation of the Serb national programme. The Church played a very

important role here, by fanning ethnic nationalism and hegemonic aspirations in the popular masses and by manipulating their religious and patriotic feelings. (Biserko 2005, 34–35)

What method of persuasion did the Serb Orthodox Church use? The intemperate use of the scapegoat ritual in political and religious discourse is the best explanation we have at this time. The Serbian Orthodox Church became the promoter of the scapegoat ritual as the dominant cultural, social, and religious motif for inciting psychological and physical violence against human beings who were not Serbs.

Walter Benjamin writes, "Fascism sees its salvation in giving these masses not their right, but instead a chance to express themselves" (2004, 255). What did the Serb Orthodox Church give the Serbian people a chance to express? It gave them a chance to express their collective trauma as victims of atrocities during World War II. The problem is that the Serb Orthdox Church gave the Serbian people a chance to express only this one thing—this sense of collective victimization—and without changing either the psychological or the sociological structure of this collective trauma (Ramet 1996). It gave the Serbian people only one way to express their collective trauma as victims in the past. This was genocide against another group of people.

In a mechanistic society, the well-being of the community takes precedence over the development of the individual. What therefore holds the society together is the solidarity of the people as a community over the solidarity of the people as individuals. As Durkheim says of mechanical solidarity, "at the moment when this solidarity exercises its force, our personality vanishes, as our definition permits us to say, for we are no longer ourselves, but the collective life" (2003, 40). This sociological notion helps describe the theological principle of *svetosavlje* (the religious rubric of Saint Sava who is the founder of the Serb Orthodox Church). As the Serb Orthodox Church pushed for a greater Serbia, they encouraged Serbian people to think no longer as individuals, but exclusively as a Serbian community. Neighbors, fellow citizens, friends, and relatives who were not Serbian were not included in this community.

Think here of the creation of Republika Srpska in Bosnia-Herzegovina after the signing of the Dayton Peace Accords. Are scapegoating, murder, rape, genocide, and sociocide effective means with which to establish a social entity? The creation of Republika Srpska is an empirical test for Girard's theory on the functional power of scapegoating. Even if Republika Srpska were established with the consent of every individual in the Serbian community, this establishment is neither viable nor sustainable.

Is there happiness in Republika Srpska today? Can there be happiness in a community whenever the madness of an ethnically pure state has been institutionalized? The political and theological position of the Serbian Orthodox Church is that now it is necessary to separate Republika Srpska from Bosnia-Herzegovina and make it a legitimate part of Serbia. The de facto situation is that Republika Srpska is indeed more connected to Serbia than to Bosnia-Herzegovina. The war crimes against Bosnian Muslims and Bosnian Croats produced the current situation, and to a significant degree the Serb Orthodox Church promoted these events.

Is *svetosavlje*, however, as an enlightened version of Serbian nationalism, a positive example of mechanical solidarity? On the surface, the answer is yes, but underneath the surface, the answer is no. Nationalism in Republika Srpska represents a negative solidarity because it is established through war crimes and crimes against humanity. To maintain this solidarity, the negativity needs to be perpetuated. The problem is that "negative solidarity does not produce any integration by itself," (Durkheim 2003, 39); Durkheim continues, "Since, moreover, there is nothing specific about it, we shall recognize only two kinds of positive solidarity [mechanical and organic]" (2003, 39). The more the Serb Orthodox Church defines the Serbian community solely through a negative relation to others, whether the Catholic Pope, Europeans, Muslims, Albanians, Communists, humanists, or atheists, the less the Serbian community is integrated.

Notice the paradox. Negative solidarity does not produce integration in that there is nothing specific about it. The specificity that the Serbian Orthodox Church claims for itself becomes insubstantial insofar as it is expressed through its antipathy and fear of what is other than itself. When the Serbian Orthodox Church defines itself in a solipsistic manner, independently of Christianity as a universal church and independently of world civilization, the Serbian Orthodox Church has nothing specific about it, despite the multiplicity of specificities that are generic to its heritage.

It is helpful now to have a clearer understanding of what sociocide is. To develop this understanding, it helps to distinguish sociocide from genocide. The argument here is that in the war against Bosnia sociocide was the end and genocide the means. In *This Time We Knew*, Tom Cushman and Stjepan Meštrović define genocide:

> Generally speaking, genocide does not necessarily mean the immediate destruction of a nation, except when accomplished by mass killings of all members of a nation. It is intended rather to signify a coordinated plan of different actions aiming at the destruction of essential foundations of the life of national groups, with the aim of annihilating the group. (1996, 359)

If genocide is a coordinated plan of different actions aiming at the destruction of the essential foundations of the life of a national group, sociocide in turn is a coordinated plan of different actions aiming at the destruction of the essential foundations of society. Jonathan Schell, as mentioned earlier, indicates how genocide leads to sociocide: "When crimes are of a certain magnitude and character, they nullify our power to respond to them adequately because they smash the human context in which human losses normally acquire their meaning for us" (1982, 145). What is the human context in which human losses acquire meaning for us? It is the social. When crimes against humanity are of a certain magnitude and character, they result in the murdering of the human context in which these losses acquire meaning for us. With the murdering of the social, crimes of a great magnitude can occur with impunity. Crimes assume a limitless character. The murdering of society necessarily accompanies war crimes, crimes against humanity, and genocide; the murdering of society is not just an unexpected upshot, but a logical consequence. Sociocide goes beyond the evil of destroying individuals, no matter how large the number. Sociocide nullifies the human ability to respond to these losses in an appropiate way because it mutilates the lifeworld that has the power to redeem the human losses suffered.

Therefore, genocide is an insufficient term to describe the consequences of armed conflict in Bosnia as well as other areas of the world today. As powerful as the term genocide is, it does not adequately encompass the consequences of what is euphemistically called "ethnic cleansing." Of course, sociocide is not a legal term. Nor is it a historically recognized crime for which one can be tried and convicted. Still, in Bosnia, genocide was a derivative consequence of sociocide.

By inverting Hegel's argument on the positive correlation between war and society, it is possible to begin to formulate the markers of sociocide. One consequence of sociocide is the dissolution of the solidarity required for society to function. Families and private communities strive exclusively after their inviolable self-existence and absolute personal security. Distrust and bad faith become the dominant orientations of human beings living together. Another consequence of sociocide is that government functions weakly, that is, bureaucratically, if at all. Social authority holds no legitimacy. It is not internalized by either individuals or groups. Another consequence of sociocide is the impossibility to restore trust and mutual confidence after the cessation of hostilities.

Žunec raises the possibility of sociocide, evoking the work of Hobbes, but he does not believe that the killing of society is truly possible:

> In the terms of Hobbes' classic philosophy of society, these wars erase the achievements of the *status civilis* and mark a return to *status naturalis*. Hobbes' Warrre, where civilization, culture, and *Society* itself disappear, has to be distinguished from war as an armed conflict in which, regardless of scope of loss of lives or material damage, *common Power* does not disappear . . . and where, regardless of the human toll, material damage, and social losses, there are no societal losses, i.e., there is no wreckage of society as such and all of its basic functions. (1999, 102)

Evil evokes the unthinkable. Today Bosnia is a protectorate. After the Dayton Peace Accord, the people with the most political power and legal legitimacy are non-Bosnians. Was the war in Bosnia tantamount to the wreckage of society and virtually all of its functions? Must the international community continue to stand in as the Common Power that was destroyed during the sociocidal war?

Hobbes says that the state of nature, where there is a war of all against all because there is no society, is an ideal type, a myth. It never existed in social history. As Žunec indicates, even during war society does not disappear. War may destroy the societal, but not society itself. The most telltale stories from Bosnia during the war were those that affirmed the interconnectedness that not only citizens but also soldiers from different sides maintained during the cruel and sadistic war they experienced. At negotiations, international diplomats were befuddled when leaders from opposing sides would meet in the evening and reminisce about friends, family, and good times. Many Bosnian Muslims fled to Belgrade for sanctuary. One of the most telltale moments in

Sheri Fink's *War Hospital: A True Story of Surgery and Survival* is when the physician with the nationalist Serb army, Dr. Boro Lazić, visits the hospital in Srebrenica under siege by Serbian forces to help evacuate wounded people. Fink writes,

They greet one another with a Balkan-style hug and kiss on both cheeks.

"How is it in Tuzla?" Nedret asks.

"I didn't come from Tuzla. . . ." Boro begins to explain.

"Ah, you're the Chetnik coming from Zvornik!" Nedret backs away from him in mock horror. "Fuck! My people will kill me!" He says it with a smile, and then invites Boro for a tour of the hospital. . . . "What's up, Boro? Oh, Boro, it's you!" People in the crowd turn their heads as Fatima approaches, smiling deliriously. Boro recognizes her from medical school, a kind and studious girl who used to lend him notes when he skipped class.

"What's up, Fata?" (2003, 186–87)

Hobbes says that the state of nature is too painful for the human species to endure. Life is short, nasty, and brutish for everyone. For Hobbes, the state of nature is simply a heuristic device, a hypothetical situation, to explain the origins and purpose of society. For us, too, sociocide is a heuristic device, a Weberian ideal type (1964, 112–15), to explain the demented and twisted orientation of contemporary war and to theorize what evil would be if it were action.

What happened in former Yugoslavia is that, in the interest of creating new nation-states, an attempt to kill Bosnian society was made. What was actually and successfully murdered was the Yugoslav federal state. It is not possible to be a Yugoslav today because the human context in which being a Yugoslav acquires meaning and significance has been destroyed. The question becomes whether these new nation-states that were established in this manner can become functional societies when the manner in which they came into existence was first to destroy the society that preceded them and on which they, too, to some degree, still depend today.

One overlooked casualty of the war in Bosnia was her collective commitment to a pluralistic, tolerant, integrated society. Unconscionable violence and vicious propaganda were brought to bear against her heritage, cultural convictions, social practices, and civic order, making it next to impossible for Bosnia to sustain her multiconfessional and syncretistic-informed traditions. Tone Bringa writes,

> Neither Bosniak, nor Croat, nor Serb identities can be fully understood with reference only to Islam or Christianity respectively, but have to be considered in a specific Bosnian context that has resulted in a shared history and locality among Bosnians of Islamic as well as Christian backgrounds. (2002, 31)

When one considers Bringa's statement, one understands that multiculturalism, in fact, is a misnomer for recounting Bosnia's heritage, even if the term is frequently used. In Bosnia, there were not multiple cultures coresiding in the same proximity; nor were there multiple cultures coexisting independently. There was a singular Bosnian culture that encompassed each ethnicity and several faiths. Christianity, Islam, and Judaism were synergistically interdependent. Bosnia was and still is a distinctly sophisticated society, and this sophistication provoked her enemies to attempt to murder her.

Distinguished scholars—Ivo Banac (1993), Tone Bringa (2002 and 1995), Robert Donia (1994), John Fine (1994), and Noel Malcolm (1994)—unequivocally assert that historically, culturally, and politically, a vibrant, noble Bosnian tradition exists. This tradition, however, is either overlooked because of misleading or inadequate education, or denied because of hostile political agendas, whether local or international. What Rusmir Mahmutćehajić (2000) calls the denial of Bosnia occurs frequently in scholarly and policy discussions. Nationalist intellectuals in Belgrade like Dobrica Ćosić and Mihailo Marković helped start the war against Bosnia by intellectualizing as if a Bosnian society never existed. This nonrecognition of Bosnia was given prominence in the local as well as global media. Robert Kaplan's ill-informed description of the area as "a land of ancient hatreds" in *Balkan Ghosts: A Journey through History* confused President Clinton and contributed to his halting policy decisions toward the evil occurring in Bosnia (Cooper 1993).

As Andras Riedlmayer's research for the Hague Tribunal incontrovertibly demonstrates, the evil of ethnic cleansing was to eradicate as completely as possible the evidence of Bosnia's heritage. The point was to destroy not only Bosnian communities (small villages, towns, and cities) with mixed populations but also the cultural material (libraries, bridges, mosques, churches, schools) that bore witness to the legacy of

Bosnia's multinational heritage. What happened in Bosnia is not just genocide, the willful destruction of the essential foundations of one particular community or group of people within a society. Of course, genocide is a distinguishing feature of the violence brought to bear against Bosnia. What happened in Bosnia is also described as sociocide, the murdering of a progressive, complex, and enlightened society in order that a regressive, simple, and bigoted society could replace it. A nation-state with a shallow, one-dimensional sense of solidarity could not be established in Croatia or Serbia when a superior model of solidarity based on pluralism and inclusiveness existed on its borders. When Serbia and Croatia were established as homogeneous nation-states based on one dominant ethnicity, the social solidarity of Bosnia, which belied the nationalistic ideologies of her neighbors, was a threat. Ivo Banac affirms this point:

> If Bosnia were a collectivity of separate entities, then it would have been a mini-Yugoslavia. But it is not that. Bosnia is a historical entity which has its own identity and its own history. . . . I view Bosnia as primarily a functioning society which Yugoslavia never was. My question is how does one keep a complicated, complex entity like Bosnia-Herzegovina together? (1993, 138–39)

What was it that made the Jerusalem-like configuration of faiths in Bosnia—Catholicism, Eastern Orthodoxy, Judaism, and Islam—vulnerable to the nationalism of her neighbors? What was it that made Bosnia's enigmatic mixture of epochs, including a distinctive, vibrant, and understudied medieval period from the thirteenth to the fifteenth century, the Ottoman Empire starting in the fifteenth century, the Austro-Hungarian Empire during the nineteenth century, and communist Yugoslavia during the twentieth century, defenseless in the face of national-state building based on a monolithic ethnicity? When one recognizes the principled, progressive character of Bosnia's tradition, recounted eloquently in the leading scholarly works on Bosnia, one would predict that Bosnia would be the last place where ethnic cleansing could have occurred with such viciousness and sadism. Within Yugoslavia, Bosnia served as a compelling model of civic order, a model that surpassed the formal model within Yugoslavia itself. Croatia and Serbia could not become the modern nation-states they wanted to be without first destroying the contrasting and threatening model on their borders.

While Bosnia is typically depicted as unconnected to Europe or undeveloped in relation to other European countries, her heritage of a pluralistic, tolerant, and open state, with a complex but singular cultural tradition, serves as an unrecognized exemplar for the European integration taking place now.

Before 1992, in the area called Republika Srpska, which is now a politically isolated part of the Republic of Bosnia-Herzegovina more connected to Serbia than to Bosnia, there were more than six hundred mosques. These were humble but majestic houses of worship constructed through the centuries with a distinct Bosnian rather than Arabic architecture. Traveling from Dubrovnik into Trebinje in 1937, Rebecca West writes in *Black Lamb and Grey Falcon: A Journey through Yugoslavia*:

> We saw the town suddenly in a parting between showers, handsome and couchant, and like all Turkish towns green with trees and refined by the minarets of many mosques. These are among the most pleasing architectural gestures ever made by urbanity. They do not publicly declare the relationship of man to God like a Christian tower or spire. They raise a white finger and say only, "This is a community of human beings and, look you, we are not beasts of the field." (1948, 271)

Trebinje is now a part of Republika Srpska, where these mosques that West saw in Trebije no longer exist. They were all destroyed after 1992 during the war. With a small degree of Serbian prejudice, West miscalls Trebinje a Turkish town when it, in fact, is a Bosnian town. West, however, astutely formulates the cultural significance of the minarets she saw, a significance shared by Bosnians, whether Muslim, Christian, or Jewish: "This is a community of human beings and look you, we are not beasts of the field" (1948, 271). Despite international pressure, hardly any of the six hundred mosques destroyed during the war in Republika Srpska have been rebuilt. The nationalistic leaders who planned and carried out ethnic cleansing in Bosnia remain in control of this region; these leaders dread the revival and recovery of the society they so ruthlessly murdered. They continuously co-opt the goodwill of international actors and leaders, who seek their insincere cooperation in a futile attempt to rebuild Bosnian society. These leaders abhor the idea of an open society within which Bosnian traditions can be revived.

The tragedy of Bosnia is that there is indeed a trans-ethnic history and a trans-ethnic culture, but today there are no viable or functional trans-ethnic institutions to support and sustain them. Tito's communism was a modern institution in which Bosnia's heritage of trans-ethnic values lived and also developed, albeit within certain limits. The best Yugoslavs, it was often said, were Bosnians. If Bosnians internalized Tito's notion of Brotherhood and Unity more easily than others, it was because Bosnians had already internalized a historical and deeper principle. Today international agencies working in Bosnia inadvertently assume a shallow, instrumental, and legalistic relation to Bosnia after which it is difficult for Bosnia to reestablish the trans-ethnic institutions it needs; the result is that Bosnia's trans-ethnic traditions, cultures, and histories are at risk.

It is helpful, therefore, to clearly distinguish sociocide from decolonization. When nationalism becomes militant, it vainly describes itself as decolonization. As Fanon (1968) describes in *The Wretched of the Earth*, the reasoning of nationalism is that the colonizers, the settlers, oppress the native community. The propaganda of Serbian nationalism constantly evokes the time of the Ottoman Empire when the empire colonized the Balkan communities they conquered. To overcome the past oppression of the Ottoman Empire, which ended over one hundred and fifty years ago, Serbian nationalism now justifies its violence against former citizens and friends in contemporary times. From the warped viewpoint of Serbian nationalists, ethnic cleansing is unfinished decolonization, however irrationally, ahistorically, unethically, and anachronistically conceived.

First, what is decolonization and how does it contrast with sociocide? Fanon writes,

> National liberation, national renaissance, the restoration of nationhood to the people, commonwealth, whatever may be the headings used or the new formulas introduced, decolonization is always a violent phenomenon. . . . Decolonization is quite simply the replacing of a certain "species" of men by another "species" of men. (1968, 35)

Notice how sociocide is different from decolonization. If decolonization is "the replacing of a certain 'species' of men by another 'species' of men,'" the replacing of the colonizers' species with the natives' species, sociocide is the destroying of the human species altogether, not only within the victims but also within the perpetrators.

It is necessary to turn to the classic writing of not only Karl Marx but also Émile Durkheim to understand what is meant by human species. For Marx, there is one species of men and women, not two or three or a thousand but one human species-being that is inherently universal and free:

> Man is a species-being, not only because in practice and in theory he adapts the species as his object (his own as well as those of other things), but—and this is only another way of expressing it—but also because he treats himself as the actual, living species; because he treats himself as a *universal* and therefore a free being. (2004, 33)

It is easier to understand what Marx means by human species-being if we replace species-being with soul. Consider the transliteration: human beings are soulful not only because in practice and in theory they adapt the soul as their object but also because human beings treat themselves as the actual, living species, as universal and consequently free beings. Replacing species-being with soul makes Marx's formulation more accessible.

Marx, of course, would object to inserting the word soul for species-being. At the same time, Marx would want to preserve the metaphysical significance of "soul" albeit within the context of a natural ontology and empirical epistemology. With Marx's notion, we have a clearer understanding of what sociocide is; it is the destruction of the human species-being such that it is essentially no different from the species of other animals. As a consequence of sociocide, the human being is "immediately identical with its life activity" (2004, 34). Like the animal, the human being does not distinguish itself from its life-activity. "It is *its life-activity*" (Marx 2004, 34).

Durkheim is clearer on this subject. He rejects Marx's sophistical notion that man is the measure of all things. In his formulation of the human species-being, Durkheim asserts that, while the measure of man is something other than man, what is other to man is neither strange nor foreign to man:

> Man's characteristic privilege is that the bond he accepts is not physical but moral; that is, social. He is governed not by a material environment brutally imposed on him, but by a conscience superior to his own, the superiority of which he feels. Because

the greater, better part of his existence transcends the body, he escapes the body's yoke, but is subject to that of society. (2004, 79)

After sociocide, after the murdering of the human species-being, the bond that human beings accept is physical, not moral. The characteristic privilege of men and women together is lost. After sociocide, human beings are governed only by the material environment and recognize no conscience other than their own. Human beings bear the body's yoke alone.

After the destruction of society, there are, of course, people, and there are, of course, people living in groups. If society no longer exists, what orientation structures the commonality of people living together? In a natural state, life is governed randomly. While randomness may be able to explain the natural order, can it explain the social order?

Anomie means that there are no social ends. Social action therefore cannot be oriented. Indeed, there cannot be social action. In the state of anomie, there are no ends from which to choose. Without the possibility of choice, action is impossible. It does not exist. The foundation for forming and carrying out decisions, for choosing between alternative ends, does not exist. If action does not exist, there can be no sociology. Sociology loses its subject and itself.

Randomness is the orientation after the death of society because randomness is the orientation of the state of nature, and randomness can neither sustain nor structure the social. Talcott Parsons argues that non-randomness must explain action and thus social order:

> For if ends are a factor at all, it must, empirically, make a difference which of two alternative ends is pursued. To pursue one of two alternative ends involves choice between them. But if the relation between these two ends is purely random there can be no choice, or rather the choice itself must be random, a result of chance. As has been noted the concept of randomness in general has no meaning, except that it is the very definition of "meaninglessness." (1968, 231)

When ends do not exist, the pseudo-end of randomness defines the situation. Randomness, however, is no end at all. In inferential statistics, this is known as the null hypothesis. The shelling, the sniping, and the killing in Bosnia were done in decidedly wanton ways to create a sense of madness among the victims. The orientation of the violence was not to be oriented. The meaningfulness of the crimes was not to represent meaningfulness.

Durkheim decries the horrendous character of a life with no effectively functioning society:

> The most blameworthy acts are so often absolved by success that the boundary between what is permitted and what is prohibited, what is just and what is unjust, has nothing fixed about it, but seems susceptible to almost arbitrary change by individuals. . . . It is this anomic state that is the cause, as we shall show, of the incessantly recurrent conflicts, and the multifarious disorders of which the economic world exhibits so sad a spectacle. . . . That such anarchy is an unhealthy phenomenon is quite evident, since it runs counter to the aim of society, which is to suppress, or at least to moderate, war among men, subordinating the law of the strongest to a higher law. To justify this chaotic state, we vainly praise its encouragement of individual liberty. (1964, 2–3)

Can this be? Can society be killed? Wherein lies the resilience of society? Society is based upon nonempirical phenomena more than modern sociology might care to admit. Just as there can be people living in a group after the death of society, there can be society after the annihilation of its living members. Society's material culture can continue to bear witness to the society that no longer is embodied by living people. Such is the case of the Beothuks (Red Indians) in Newfoundland, Canada. Individuals from this native community were murdered; diseases from Europe killed the rest. The genocide the Beothuks suffered was total. None of their relatively small population survived. When one visits Newfoundland, however, one witnesses that they still exist not just empirically through their remains and artifacts, but also metaphysically through the mere saying of their name and the telling of their story among those now living in Newfoundland (Marshall 1996).

The Dayton Peace Accords stopped a horrible war; it was an historic event. The Dayton Peace Accords, however, is now used as another weapon in the hands of nationalist politicians who want to kill the Bosnian spirit and the country that cherishes this spirit. The longer Bosnia remains divided as two autonomous entities, the more likely the desires of nationalist politicians on all sides will be realized. The longer Ratko Mladić and Radovan Karadžić remain un-arrested, the more likely their goal of destroying Bosnia will be achieved. In *Genocide in Bosnia: The Policy of "Ethnic Cleansing,"* Norman Cigar concludes his study by pointing out the broader significance of his subject: "Ultimately, the greatest cost of genocide in Bosnia-Herzegovina may well be to the world's value system. In moral terms, this case implies a disturbing vision of the future" (Cigar 1995, 200).

The conclusion of Cigar's study constitutes the beginning of this one. When society accepts genocide as an efficient means to a particular end, the predictable consequence is sociocide.

Lilies

In both field and mountain the white lilies
    have bloomed
So in field and mountain the lily seems to
    speak
In mount and dale every lily
Seems to blaze
And when so pensive among the blooming
    flowers
You silently
Pass
Maybe like me you think of those
Who passed silently by here
Before you
Among the blooming white flowers
Wondering just as you do
What are these white
Lilies
Are they someone's rejoicings
Or
Wailings
The signs of those who once passed
In these pathless regions and
Hopelessly
Trod
In search of white flowers

    —Mak Dizdar
Translated by Omer Hadžiselimović

References

Agee, Chris, ed. 1998. *Scar on the stone: Contemporary poetry from Bosnia.* Newcastle, England: Bloodaxe Books.
Alexander, Jeffrey C. 2001. Toward a sociology of evil: Getting beyond modernist common sense about the alternative to "the good." In *Rethinking evil: Contemporary perspectives*, edited by María Pía Lara, 153–72. Berkeley: University of California Press.
Ali, Rabia, and Lawrence Lifschultz, eds. 1993. *Why Bosnia?: Writings on the Balkan war.* Stony Creek, Conn.: Pamphleteer's Press.
Andrić, Ivo. 1977. *The bridge on the Drina.* Translated by Lovett F. Edwards. Chicago: University of Chicago Press.
Aristotle. 1962. *Nicomachean ethics.* Translated by Martin Ostwald. Indianapolis: Bobbs-Merrill.
Bakhtin, Mikhail. 1984. *Problems of Dostoyevsky's poetics.* Translated by R. W. Rotsel. Minneapolis: University of Minnesota Press.
———. 1996. *The dialogic imagination.* Edited by Michael Holquist and translated by Caryl Emerson and Michael Holquist. Austin: University of Texas Press.
Banac, Ivo. 1993. Separating history from myth: An interview with Ivo Banac. In *Why Bosnia? Writings on the balkan war*, edited by Rabia Ali and Lawrence Lifschultz, 134–64. Stony Creek, Conn.: Pamphleteer's Press.
Bataille, Georges. 1973. *Literature and evil.* Translated by Alastair Hamilton. London: Calder and Boyars.
Baudrillard, Jean. 1995. *The Gulf war did not take place.* Translated by Paul Patton. Bloomington: Indiana University Press.
———. 1999. *Fatal strategies.* Translated by Philip Beitchman and W. G. J. Niesluchowski. London: Pluto Press.
———. 2004. Simulacra and simulations: Disneyland. In *Social theory: The multicultural and classic readings*, edited by Charles Lemert, 471–76. Boulder, Colo.: Westview.

Bellah, Robert N., Richard Madsen, William M. Sullivan, Ann Swidler, and Steven M. Tipton. 1985. *Habits of the heart: Individualism and commitment in American life*. New York: Harper and Row.
Benjamin, Walter. 2004. Art, war, and fascism. In *Social theory: The multicultural and classic readings*, edited by Charles Lemert, 255–56. Boulder, Colo.: Westview.
Bernstein, Richard. 1996. *Hannah Arendt and the Jewish question*. Cambridge, Mass.: MIT Press.
———. 2002. *Radical evil: A philosophical investigation*. Malden, Mass.: Blackwell Publishing Polity.
Biserko, Sonja. 2005. Serbia in the thrall of dogmatic thinking—the outcome of a failed project. *Bosnia Report* 45–46 (May–August): 33–39.
Blum, Alan. 1978. *Socrates: The original and its images*. London: Routledge and Kegan Paul.
Borden, Anthony. 2001. Milošević's fate in the balance. *Balkan Crises Report* 232 (March 31), http://www.iwpr.net/index.php?apc_state=hen&s=o&o=archive/bcr/bcr_2 0 010331_2_eng.txt (accessed December 30, 2005).
Bringa, Tone. 1995. *Being Muslim the Bosnian way: Identity and community in a central Bosnian village*. Princeton: Princeton University Press.
———. 2002. Islam and the quest for identity in post-communist Bosnia-Herzegovina. In *Islam and Bosnia: Conflict resolution and foreign policy in multi-ethnic states*, edited by Maya Shatzmiller, 24–34. Montreal: McGill-Queen's University Press.
Broz, Svetlana. 2004. *Good people in an evil time: Portraits of complicity and resistance in the Bosnian war*. Translated by Ellen Elias-Bursać. New York: Other Press.
Buber, Martin. 1956. Good and evil. In *The writings of Martin Buber*, edited by Will Herberg, 89–96. New York: Meridian Books.
———. 1958. *I and thou*. Translated by Ronald Gregor Smith. New York: Macmillan.
Burke, Kenneth. 1969. *A grammar of motives*. Berkeley: University of California Press.
Butler, Thomas. 2001. "The Hagueing of Slobodan Milošević and the struggle for the soul of Serbia." Unpublished manuscript (cited with author's permission).
Carens, Joseph H, ed. 1993. *Democracy and possessive individualism: The intellectual legacy of C. B. Macpherson*. Albany, N.Y.: State University of New York Press.
———. 1993. Exchange. *Times Literary Supplement* 4711 (July 16): 15–16.
Čekić, Smail, Muharem Kreso, and Bećir Macić. 2001. *Genocide in Srebrenica, United Nations "Safe Area" in July 1995*. Sarajevo: Institute for the Research of Crimes against Humanity and International Law.
Cigar, Norman. 1995. *Genocide in Bosnia: The policy of "ethnic cleansing."* College Station: Texas A&M University Press.
Čolović, Ivan. 2002. *The politics of symbol in Serbia: Essays in political anthropology*. London: Hurst.
Cooley, Charles. 1962. *Social organization: A study of the larger mind*. New York: Schocken Books.

Cooper, Henry R. Jr. 1993. Review of *Balkan ghosts: A journey through history* by Robert D. Kaplan. *Slavic Review* 52 (fall): 592–93.
Crocker, David A. 1977. Marković's concept of *praxis* as norm. *Inquiry* 20: 1–43.
———. 1983. *Praxis and democratic socialism: The critical theory of Marković and Stojanović.* New Jersey: Humanities Press.
———. 1981. Marković on critical social theory and human nature. In *Marxism and the good society*, edited by J. P. Burke, 157–81. Cambridge: Cambridge University Press.
Cushman, Thomas. 2000. The sociology of evil and the destruction of Bosnia. *Hedgehog Review: Critical Reflections on Contemporary Culture* 2 (summer): 29–43.
Cushman, Tom, and Stjepan Meštrović, eds. 1996. *This time we knew: Western responses to genocide in Bosnia.* New York: University Press.
Djordjević, Mirko. 1996. Serbia's ark in the eye of the storm. *Warreport* 40 (April): 28–30.
Doder, Dusko. 1993. Serbia's academic apologist. *Chronicle of Higher Education.* April 7.
Donia, Robert J., and John V. A. Fine. 1994. *Bosnia and Hercegovina: A tradition betrayed.* New York: Columbia University Press.
Doubt, Keith. 1999. O nepravdi postmodernism: Peter Handke o Srbiji i lekcija iz Bosne [On the injustice of postmodernism: Peter Handke on Serbia and a lesson from Bosnia]. *Novi Izraz* 3 (spring): 91–101.
———. 2000. O latentnoj funkciji etničkog čišćenja u Bosni [On the latent function of ethnic cleansing in Bosnia]. *Forum Bosnae* 7–8: 22–37.
———. 2000. *Sociology after Bosnia and Kosovo: Recovering justice.* Lanham, Md.: Rowman and Littlefield.
———. 2001. O upotrebi dvoličnog diskursa u globalnim medijima od strane počinitelja rathih zločina u Bosni [On the double-voiced discourse in the global media by perpetrators of war crimes in Bosnia]. *Odjek* 1 (spring–summer): 9–14.
———. 2002. "Civilno društvo na Balkanu" [Civil society in the Balkans], *Odjek* (spring–summer): 39–40.
———. 2002. Intellektualna izdaja i Bosanskohercegovačka muka [Intellectual betrayal and Bosnia-Hercegovina's suffering]. *Odjek* (fall–winter): 56–64.
———. 2002. What is the evil of war crimes? The ethical requirement of burial and its transgression in the war in Bosnia-Herzegovina. *Peace, Conflict, and Development* 1 (June), http://www.peacestudiesjournal.org.uk/index.asp (accessed December 30, 2006).
———. 2003. *Sociologija nakon Bosne* [Sociology after Bosnia]. Sarajevo: Buybook.
———. 2004. Evil and the ritual of shame: A crime against humanity in Bosnia-Herzegovina. *Janus Head* 7, no. 3: 319–31.
———. 2004. Socratic medicine for Radovan Karadžić. *Odjek* (autumn–winter): 32–37, http://www.odjek.ba/eng/index.php?broj=02&id=07 (accessed December 14, 2005).
———. 2004. Last words/first words. *Odjek* (autumn–winter): 99–100, http://www.odjek.ba/eng/index.php?broj=02&id=26 (accessed December 14, 2005).

Durkheim, Émile. 1915. *The elementary forms of religious life*. New York: Free Press.
———. 1964. *The division of labor in society*. Translated by George Simpson. New York: Free Press.
———. 1973. Individualism and the intellectuals. In *On morality and society*, edited by Robert Bellah. Chicago: University of Chicago Press.
———. 1975. *Durkheim on religion*, edited by W. S. F. Pickering. New York. Oxford University Press.
———. 2003. On Mechanical and Organic Solidarity. In *Social Theory: Roots and Branches*, edited by Peter Kivisto, 38–42. Los Angeles, Calif.: Roxbury Publishing Company.
Fanon, Fanz. 1968. *The wretched of the earth*. Translated by Constance Farrington. New York: Grove Press.
Fink, Sheri. 2003. *War hospital: A true story of surgery and survival*. New York: Public Affairs.
Fromm, Erich. 1974. Foreword to *From affluence to praxis: Philosophy and social criticism*, by Marković Mihailo. Ann Arbor: University of Michigan Press
Gaita, Raymond. 1998. *A common humanity: Thinking about love and truth and justice*. London: Routledge.
Garfinkel, Harold. 1956. Conditions of successful degradation ceremonies. *American Journal of Sociology* 61: 420–24.
Girard, René. 1972. *Violence and the sacred*. Baltimore: John Hopkins.
Gjelten, Tom. 1997. Reviving historical hatred. *Washington Post* July 6, http: // www.washingtonpost.com / wp-srv / style / longterm / books / reviews / serbs.htm (accessed December 30, 2005).
Gow, James. 2003. *The Serbian project and its adversaries: A strategy of war crimes*. Montreal: McGill-Queen's University Press.
Gruenwald, Oskar. 1983. *The Yugoslav search for man: Marxist humanism in contemporary Yugoslavia*. South Hadley, Mass.: J. F. Bergin.
Gunić, Vehid. 2001. *Shame on you, Europe*. Sarajevo: Planijax.
Halsell, Grace. 1993. Women's bodies: A battlefield in war for Greater Serbia. *Washington Report on Middle East Affairs*, April–May, http://www.washington-report.org/backissues/0493/9304008.htm (accessed December 31, 2005).
Handke, Peter. 1997. *A journey to the rivers: Justice for Serbia*. Translated by Scott Abbott. New York: Viking.
Hastings, Adrian. 1994. *SOS Bosnia*, 3d ed. Leeds, England: Margaret Fenton Ltd.
Hayden, Robert M. 1995. Focus: Constitutionalism and nationalism in the Balkans. *East European Constitutional Review* 5 (fall): 68–75.
Hegel, G. W. F. 1977. *The phenomenology of mind*. Translated by J. B. Baillie. New York: Humanities Press.
Heidegger, Martin. 1971. *Poetry, language, thought*. Translated by Albert Hofstadter New York: Harper and Row.
Hemon, Aleksandar. 2005. The Srebrenica web. *Bosnia Report* 45–46 (May–August): 1–2.

Hobbes, Thomas. 1968. *Leviathan*, edited by by C. B. Macpherson. Middlesex, England: Penguin.
Honig, Jan W., and Norbert Both. 1996. *Srebrenica: Record of a war crime*. Middlesex, England: Penguin.
Jagger, Bianca. 1995. The betrayal of Srebrenica. *European*. September 25–October 1, http://www.haverford.edu/rlg/sells/srebrenica/BiancaJagger1.html (accessed December 31, 2005).
Kant, Immanuel. 1917. *Perpetual peace: A philosophical essay*. London: George Allen and Unwin.
Kinzer, Stephen. 1992. A sort of "super Serb" defends Serbian policy. *New York Times*, August 26, http://lexis-nexis.com/.
Kiš, Danilo. 1993. "Nationalism." In *Why Bosnia? Writings on the Balkan war*, edited by Rabia Ali and Lawrence Lifschultz, 126–28. Stony Creek, Conn.: Pamphleteer's Press.
Klein, Jacob. 1977. *Plato's trilogy: Theaetetus, the Sophist and the Statesman*. Chicago: University of Chicago Press.
Kluckhohn, Clyde. 1964. *Culture and behavior*. Glencoe, Ill.: Free Press.
Kroeber, A. L. 1923. *Anthropology*. New York: Harcourt, Brace.
Kurspahić, Kemal. 1997. *As long as Sarajevo exists*. Translated by Colleen London. Stony Creek, Conn.: Pamphleteer's Press.
Le Bon, Gustave. 1982. *The crowd: A study of the popular mind*. Marietta, Ga.: Larlin.
Levinas, Emmanuel. 1985. *Ethics and infinity: Conversations with Philippe Nemo*. Translated by Richard A. Cohen. Pittsburgh, Penn.: Duquesne University Press.
———. 1989. *The Levinas reader*, edited by Seán Hand. Oxford: Blackwell.
Little, Allan. 2001. The West did not do enough. *BBC News*. June 29, http://news.bbc.co.uk/1/hi/programmes/from_our_own_correspondent/1413764.stm (accessed December 29, 2005).
Maass, Peter. 1997. *Love thy neighbor: A story of war*. New York: Vintage Books.
Magaš, Branka. 1993. *The destruction of Yugoslavia: Tracking the break-up 1980–92*. London: Verso.
Mahmutćehajić, Rusmir. 2000. *The denial of Bosnia*. Translated by Francis R. Jones and Marina Bowder. University Park: Pennsylvania State University Press.
Malcolm, Noel. 1994. *Bosnia: A short history*. New York: New York University Press.
Malinowski, Bronislaw. 1954. *Magic, science, and religion*. New York: Doubleday Anchor Books.
Marković, Mihailo. 1966. Humanism and dialectic. In *Socialist humanism: An international symposium*, edited by Erich Fromm, 84–97. Garden City, N.Y.: Anchor Books.
———. 1993. Exchange. *Times Literary Supplement* 4711 (July 16): 15–16.
Marshall, Ingeborg. 1996. *A history and ethnography of the Beothuk*. Montreal: McGill-Queen's University Press.
Marx, Karl. 2004. Estranged labor. In *Social theory: The multicultural and classic readings*, edited by Charles Lemert, 30–36. Boulder, Colo.: Westview.

McBride, William L. 2001. Marković's language and the spirit of community. In *From Yugoslav praxis to global pathos: Anti-hegemonic post-post-Marxist essays*, 31–40. Lanham, Md.: Rowman and Littlefield.

Mead, George H. 1934. *Mind, self, and society: From the standpoint of a social behaviorist*. Chicago: University of Chicago Press.

———. 1956. *On social psychology: Selected papers*, edited by Anselm Strauss. Chicago: University of Chicago Press.

Mehmedinović, Semezdin. 1998. *Sarajevo blues*. Translated by Ammiel Alcaley. San Francisco: City Lights.

Merton, Robert K. 1968. Manifest and latent functions. In *Social theory and social structure: Toward the codification of theory and research*, 21–83. New York: Free Press.

Mešinović, Sabahudin. 1993. *Bosnia: Testament to war crimes as told by survivors*, edited by Alijah Gordon. Malaysia: Malaysian Sociological Research Institute.

Mirsada. 1997. Testimonies of rape. *Women for women in Bosnia: Testimonies*. http:/ /www.embassy.org/wmn4wmn/personal.html (accessed December 15, 1997; site now discontinued).

Morrow, Lance. 2002. *Evil: An investigation*. New York: Basic Books.

Nietzsche, Friedrich. 1967. *On the geneology of morals*. New York: Vintage.

Parsons, Talcott. 1968. *The structure of social action: A study in social theory with special reference to a group of recent European writers*. New York: Free Press.

Plato. 1960. *Gorgias*. Translated by Walter Hamilton. Middlesex, England: Penguin.

———. 1968. *The republic of Plato*. Translated by Allan Bloom. New York: Basic Books.

———. 1975. *Protagoras and Meno*. Translated by W. K. C. Guthrie. Baltimore: Penguin.

Radić, Radmila. 2000. The Church and the "Serbian question." In *The Road to War in Serbia: Trauma and Catharsis*, edited by Nebojša Popov, 247–73. Budapest: Central European University Press.

Ramet, Sabrina. 1996. Nationalism and the "idiocy" of the countryside: The case of Serbia. *Ethnic and Racial Studies* 19 (January): 70–87.

Rohde, David. 1997. *Endgame: The betrayal and fall of Srebrenica, Europe's worst massacre since World War II*. New York: Farrar, Straus, and Giroux.

Said, Edward W. 1995. *Orientalism: Western conceptions of the orient*. London: Penguin.

Sartre, Jean-Paul. 1965. *Anti-Semite and Jew*. Translated by George J. Becker. New York: Schocken Books.

Schell, Jonathan. 1982. *The fate of the earth*. New York: Knopf.

Schneider, Peter. 1997. A writer takes a hike. *New Republic* (March) 3: 34–38.

Schultz, Alfred. 1955. On multiple realities. *Philosophy and Phenomenological Research* 5: 543–52.

Secor, Laura. 1999. Testaments betrayed: Yugoslavian intellectuals and the road to war. *Lingua Franca* 9 (September), http://www.linguafranca.com/9909/testbet.html (accessed December 15, 2000; site now discontinued).

Sells, Michael A. 1996. *The bridge betrayed: Religion and genocide in Bosnia*. Berkeley: University of California Press.

Sher, Gerson S. 1977. *Praxis: Marxist criticism and dissent in socialist Yugoslavia*. Bloomington: Indiana University Press.
Silber, Laura, and Alan Little. 1996. *Yugoslavia: Death of a nation*. New York: TV Books.
Simmel, Georg. 1950. *The sociology of Georg Simmel*, edited by Kurt H. Wolff. Glencoe, Ill.: Free Press.
Snyder, Mark. 1987. *Public appearances, private realities: The psychology of self-monitoring*. New York: W. H. Freeman.
Solecki, Ralph S. 1971. *Shanidar: The first flower people*. New York: Knopf.
Todorova, Maria. 1997. *Imagining the Balkans*. New York: Oxford University Press.
Van de Roer, Robert. 1998. "Doormodderen is een prestatie" [Muddling on is an achievement]. *NRC Handlesblad*, April 25, http://listserv.buffa lo.edu/cgi-bin/wa?A2=ind9811&L=justwatch-l&D=0&P= 1992 (accessed December 31, 2005).
Vukić, Snjezana. 1995. Refugees tell of woman singled out for rape. *Independent*, July 18.
Vygotsky, L. S. 1962. *Thought and language*. Translated by Eugenia Hanfmann and Gertrude Vakar. Cambridge, Mass.: MIT Press.
Weber, Max. 1958. *From Max Weber*, edited by H. H. Gerth and C. Wright Mills. New York: Oxford University Press.
———. 1964. *The theory of social and economic organization*, edited by Talcott Parsons and translated by A. M. Henderson and Talcott Parsons. New York: Free Press.
West, Rebecca. 1948. *Black lamb and grey falcon: A journey through Yugoslavia*. New York: Penguin Books.
Wolin, Richard. 1993. French Heidegger wars. In *The Heidegger controversy: A critical reader*, edited by Richard Wolin, 273–300. Cambridge, Mass.: MIT Press.
Žižek, Slavoj. 1996. Sex in the age of virtual reality. *Science as Culture* 5, no. 4: 506–25.
Zulfikarpašić, Adil. 1998. *The Bosniak: Adil Zulfikarpašić in dialogue with Milovan Djilas and Nadežda Gaće*. London: Hurst.
Žunec, Ozren. 1999. Ethnic rallying in Bosnia and Herzegovina: The Hobbesian account. *Sociological Imagination* 36 (2–3): 94–108.

VIDEO DOCUMENTARIES

A cry from the grave. VHS. Directed by Leslie Woodhead. London: Antelope, 1999.
Calling the ghosts. VHS. Produced by Mandy Jacobson and Karmen Jelinčić. Distributed by Women Make Movies. New York: Bowery Productions, 1996.
Killing memory: Bosnia's cultural heritage and its destruction. VHS. Produced and narrated by András Riedlmayer. Haverford, Penn.: Community of Bosnia Foundation, 1994.
Serbian epics. VHS. Directed by Pawel Pawlikowski. London: BBC TV, 1992.

Siege of Sarajevo: 1992–1996. VHS. Edited by Suada Kapić. Sarajevo: FAMA, 2000.
We are all neighbors. VHS. Directed by Debbie Christie with Tone Bringa. Chicago: Public Media, Inc., and Films, Inc., 1993.
Yugoslavia: Death of a nation. VHS. New York: Discovery Channel, 1995.

Index

action
  contrasted to behavior, 5 6, 12, 28, 31, 89, 99
  elements of
    actor, 4–6, 13, 26, 109, 122–23, 131
    conditions, 5, 7, 18, 29–31, 59, 69, 74
    end, 3–4, 14, 108, 111, 126, 134
    means 4–5, 7, 13, 27, 44, 98, 108, 122, 124, 136
    normative orientation, 4–7, 10, 12, 29–30, 46–47, 51, 69, 72–73, 78, 85, 108, 122
    role of choice, 5–6, 31, 50–51, 59, 77, 112, 134
  funeral service, as example of, 17–21
  as nonrandom
    in postmodernism, 67–68, 72–73, 77
    in Parson's theory of action, 133–34
    in Hobbes' theorizing, 50
  in relation to evil
    Alexandar, 111
    Bataille, 111
    Baudrillard, 25, 91
    Buber, 8, 65, 107
    Cushman, 111
    Gow, 122–23
    Žižek, 112
  as subject of social science
    history, 4, 6
    philosophy, 5–6, 50
    political science, 4–5
    psychology, 5, 81, 96
    sociology, 4–5, 48, 96–98, 134–35
  theory of,
    Aristotle, 3, 108, 120
    Burke, 4
    Parsons, 4–5, 73, 123, 134
Akashi Yasushi, observations of Karadžić, 84
Alexandar, Jeffrey, 111
Andrić, Ivo
  Bridge on the Drina, 101
  scapegoating of Radosav 101
animals, contrasted to humans, 6, 19, 133
anomie, 29–30, 100, 134
anti-Semitism, 59, 81–82, 91–93, 105
Arendt, Hannah, on banality of evil, 110
Aristotle, 3–4, 108, 120

bad faith, 29, 49, 59–60, 105, 113, 127

Bakhtin, Mikhail, 53
   on double-voiced discourse, 53, 55, 59
Balkans, Europe's relation to, 91–94, 100–1, 105
Banac, Ivo, on Bosnia-Herzegovina, 45, 129, 130
Bataille, Georges, overlooking Socratic position on evil, 111
Baudrillard, Jean, 25, 55–56, 91
Benjamin, Walter, on fascism, 68, 124
Bernstein, Richard, 40, 50, 119
blushing, as self-consciousness, 83–84, 113–15, 118
Bosnia
   cultural heritage, 25–26, 45, 132
   history, 43, 71, 130–32
   model of civil order in Yugoslavia, 7, 116–17, 128–32
Bridge on the Drina, 101
Bringa, Tone, 20, 45, 119, 129
Buber, Martin, 8, 34, 65, 81, 107
burial ceremony, 16–21, 116–17, 122
   as formulated by
      Durkheim, 17–18
      Hegel, 19
      Kluckhohn, 17, 19
      Kroeber, 18–19
      Solecki, 18
Burke, Kenneth
   on action, 4
   on scapegoating, 101–2

Calling the Ghosts, 37–38
Carens Josephs, 41–42
choice, as element of action, 5–6, 31, 50–51, 59, 77, 112, 134
Cigar, Norman, 123, 136
Čolović, Ivan, 50–51
confronting evil, 7, 15, 33, 38, 50–51, 60, 74, 80, 82–87, 96, 113
conscience, 9–10, 34, 59, 99, 110, 114, 133–34
   verses self-consciousness, 74–78, 82, 87
   of world, 6, 17, 21–25, 30–34, 38, 52–53, 56–60, 67, 80, 87–89, 103, 110, 115, 117–18, 136

crowd, 12–13, 54–55. *See* LeBon, Gustave
Cry from the Grave, 21
Cushman, Thomas, 111, 126

Dayton Peace Accords, critique of, 14, 106, 124, 127, 135
decolonization, contrasted to sociocide, 132
Derrida, Jacques, 50, 65
Dizdar, Mak
   "Sea," 1
   "Paths," 63–64
   "Lilies," 137
Djilas, Aleska, on scapegoating Milošević, 95–96, 102
Drina River, as trope for postmodern divinity, 72–74
Durkheim, Émile
   on Dreyfus affair, 105
   on duty of burial service, 17–18
   on species-being, 17–18, 133
   on impunity and moral disorder, 135
   on individual human rights and social order, 105–6
   mechanical solidarity, 48, 125
   negative solidarity, 125
   organic solidarity, 48, 125
   contrasted with Hobbes, 105

empiricism, independent of metaphysics, 6–7, 40, 46–47, 50, 72, 81, 88, 105, 123, 133, 135
ethical irrationality of the world, 9, 49, 75–76, 98, 105, 132
ethnic cleansing
   aim of, 12–13, 28
   as degradation ceremony, 26, 28–34
   as euphemism, 8, 113, 126
   latent function of, 9–10, 14, 34, 57, 101, 122
   manifest function of, 9, 13–14, 57
evil
   abuse of language, 52–61
   as action, 3–4, 7, 56–57, 107–13, 120, 122–23, 126, 134–36
   consciousness of another through projection, 31, 54–58, 69–70, 93–94, 96–97, 102–3

defilement of humanity, 7, 20, 32–36, 45, 60–61, 74, 77–78, 86–87, 100, 105, 110, 114, 122–26
exploitation of witness, 27–34, 37, 56–58, 120
as good-in-itself, 111–12
intellectual support of, 39–51
moral response to, 6, 59, 74–75, 78–79, 100, 105, 116, 123, 135–36
as radical, 21–22, 110–14
as ritual
  degradation ceremony, 26–34
  scapegoating, 93–106
as shameless, 15, 84, 87
as sociocide, 22, 113, 120, 124–26, 130, 132–36
Socratic position, 3–4, 7, 107–15
as unintelligible, 15, 28–29, 49, 110–15, 126

Fanon, Franz, 132
Funeral, 16–21, 116–17, 122. *See also* burial ceremony

Garfinkel, Harold, 26, 28–31, 33
genocide, 21–22, 44, 50, 77, 96, 102–5, 111, 113, 120, 124–30, 135–36
  Beothuks in Newfoundland, 135
  contrasted to sociocide, 21–22, 120, 124–36
Girard, René
  on envy, 99
  juxtaposed to Hobbes, 97–100
  on scapegoating, 97–99, 124–25
good, as end of action, 3–4, 13, 49, 75, 108–14, 120, 123
Gorgias, 65, 76–77, 107–8, 113
Gow, James, on Serbian war strategy, 122–23
Gunić, Vehid, on misrepresentation of massacre at Vase Miskina Street, 56

Habits of the Heart, 121
Handke, Peter
  sympathy for Serbian position, 66–78
  Drina River as trope, 72–73
  narrative as picture-taking, 66–68, 71–72
  postmodern notion of justice, 73–79
Hayden, Robert, critique of Dayton Peace Accord, 106
Hegel, G. W. F.
  on divine law, as inherent to nationalism, 116
  on positive reason for war, 121, 126–27
  on spiritual function of funeral, 19–20
Heidegger Martin
  on language, 52, 61
  Nazi involvement, 49–50
Hobbes, Thomas
  account of social order, 7, 18, 29–30, 97–99, 127–28
  compared to Durkheim, 105–6
  contrasted with Girard, 97–99
Holocaust, 7
human nature, 18–22, 36–40, 46, 99, 132–34
  as formulated by Cooley, 15
  as species-being, 18–22, 34, 36–40, 46, 99, 132–34
  Durkheim, 133–34
  Marx, 18, 34, 36, 40, 46, 133–34
  as spiritual, 34, 81, 113–14, 141
human rights, as foundation of social order, 100, 105–6

Imagining the Balkans, 91–93
intellectual betrayal, 41, 45–6, 122

justice , 4, 47–49, 73–79, 113–17
  for victims, 21–22, 57–58, 76–79, 115, 118, 124, 132
  for victimizers, 76–79, 113–17, 132
  injustice, 35–36, 57–58, 73–79, 96–97, 134–35
  injustice of justice for war criminals, 76–79

Kandić, Nataša, 102
Karadžić, Radovan
  observed by Zulfikarpašić, 109–110

as charismatic figure, 83, 85–87, 89
as evil agent, 4, 60, 76–77, 82–87, 107–18
as motivated actor, 107–18
pre-war speech in Zvornik, 109–10
political background in Sarajevo, 82–83
observed by Mehmedinović, 82–83, 112
in *Serbian Epics*, 84
as someone who blushes, 83–84, 87, 113–15, 117–18
observed by Yasushi Akashi, 84
Karremans, Ton, 104–5
Kiš, Danilo
on nationalism, 80–83, 88–89
use of Sartre, 81–83, 88–89
Kluckhorn, Clyde, on burial ceremony, 17, 19
Kroeber, A. L., on burial ceremony, 18–19

LeBon, Gustave, 12

Maass, Peter, 10–11, 13, 26–27
Malcolm, Noel, 9, 45, 129
Malinowski, Bronislaw, on funeral 20, 22–23
Marković, Mihailo
biography, 39–40
observed by Čolović, 50–51
critical theory's responsibility toward, 45, 49–51
extent literature, 40, 44
political activity compared to Heidegger's Nazi involvement, 49–50
on *praxis*, 40, 44, 46–49
as propagandist for Serbian nationalism, 41–44
in contrast to Protagoras, 47–49
on Serbian nationalism, 41–42, 45, 50–51
support from Fromm, 40
Marx, Karl, on species-being, 18, 34, 36, 40, 46, 133
mass graves, as misnomer, 16,
Mead, George Herbert,

avoidance of metaphysical question, 88
"I" of self, 81–84, 88
"Me" of self, 81–84, 88–89
contrasted to Vygotsky, 88–89
mechanical solidarity, 48, 124–25. See also *svetosavlje*
Mehmedinović, Senezdin, account of Karadžić, 82, 84–85, 112
Merton, Robert K.
on latent function, 8–10, 14–15, 122
on manifest function, 9, 13–14
on objectivity in functional analysis. 9
Milošević, Slobodan
use of double-voiced discourse, 52–55, 66–67, 94–95
observed by Mitević, 54, 94–95
Mihailo Marković's support of, 40–41, 44
as leader who scapegoats, 9–10, 12, 40–41, 45, 94–95
as scapegoat at Hague, 87, 95–96, 102, 115
scapegoating of Azem, 54, 94–95
as war criminal, 45–46, 121, 123
Mladić, Ratko
as high self-monitor, 89–90
"gift" to Serbian people, 59–61
manipulation of United Nations, 103–4
as fallacious representation of natural right, 76–78
moral dissonance, 32, 74, 101. See blushing
Morrow, Lance, on shamelessness of evil, 15

nationalism
compared to anti-Semitism, 59–61, 81–95
co-optation of righteousness, 32, 54, 57, 95–96, 103
as crowd-like, 12–13, 54–55
as decolonization, 132
manipulation of world, 33–34
suppression of human law, 116–17
negative solidarity, as consequence of scapegoating, 125

normative orientation, as element of social action, 4–7, 10, 12, 29–30, 46–7, 51, 69, 72–73, 78, 85, 108, 122
Notes from the Underground, 53

organic solidarity, 48, 125
Orientalism, 92

Parsons, Talcott,
  on randomness, 134–35
  Structure of Social Action, 4–5, 73, 123, 134–35
Plato
  "Divided Line," 6–7
  Gorgias, 65, 76–77, 107–9, 113
  Protagoras, 47–49
  Republic, 7–7, 65, 113–15
  Thrasymachus's blushing, 113–15
polyphonic discourse, 57, 58, 60. *See* Bakhtin, Mihail
postmodern epistemology, 67–68, 93
power, social construction of, 27, 53–54, 86–87, 95–96, 102–3
praxis,
  in contrast to alienation, 40, 46–49
  in relation to species-being, 46–49
Protagoras, on inter-dependency of virtues, 47–49

radical evil, as untenable position, 110, 112–14
Raguž, Vlado, in *Siege of Sarajevo*, 17
Ramet, Sabrina, 123–24
randomness, in state of nature, 50, 66–68, 72–73, 77, 134–35
rape
  as assault on self, 26, 35–36
  transgression of species-being, 36–38
  as war crime, 37
Reidlmajer, Andras, 25
Republika Srpksa, 85 87, 115, 124–25, 131
resilience of human spirit, 22, 34, 135
role reversal of witness with victim, 30–34, 84–85

Said, Edward, 92
Sarajevo, preservation of ethical order under siege, 17
Sartre, Jean-Paul, on anti-Semitism, 59, 81
scapegoating
  Andrić, 101
  as Balkan pathology, 93–96
  as barbarity, 100
  problem of collective guilt, 9–10, 34, 95, 102
  Durkheim, 105–6
  Girard, 97–99
  in literature, 100–1
  psychological account, 96–97
  sociological account, 97–101
  theological account, 100
  as vicarious atonement, 101–2
  See also Milošević, Slobodan
Schell, Jonathan, on evil's destructiveness, 21–22, 126
Schultz, Alfred, 28–29
Scorpion video, as snuff film, 102–3
self-consciousness,
  of barbarian, 87–88
  blush, 83–84, 113–15, 118
  in burial ceremony, 18–20, 24
  in contrast to conscience, 74–79, 82
  of human spirit, 36, 38
  of nationalist Serbs, 53–55, 70–74
Serbian Epics, 84
Serbian Orthodox Church
  use of scapegoating, 123–25
  manipulation of Serbian people, 90, 115–17, 123–25
  political use of burial ceremony, 115–17
svetosavlje, 124–25
Serbian people
  Handke's sympathy for, 66–75,
  manipulation of, 12–13, 32, 34, 41, 43, 45, 50–51, 56–61, 78, 84, 90, 95–96, 101–3, 115–17, 122–24, 132
shame
  and evil, 15, 29, 30, 33, 84, 87
  and charisma, 83, 85–90

shamelessness, 84
Siege of Sarajevo, 17
Simmel, Georg, 70, 75
social contract, contrasted to Girard's account of scapegoating, 97–100
sociocide
   consequences of, 22, 43, 57, 77, 113, 124–36
   juxtaposed to decolonization, 132
   defined, 22, 120–21, 125–36
   as evil, 22, 57, 71, 124–36
   juxtaposed to genocide, 22, 125–36
sociology, as science of action, 4–5, 48, 97, 134–35
Socrates
   on evil, 3–4, 7, 76–77, 108–14
   opposition to Socratic position, 65, 110–14
   refutation of Polus, 76–79, 107–9
   refutation of Protagoras, 47–49
Solecki, Ralph S., 18
Sophie's Choice, 112
species-being
   as formulated by
      Durkheim, 17–18, 105–6, 133
      Marx, 18, 34, 36, 40, 46, 133
   juxtaposed to soul, 133
Srebrenica, 11–14, 21, 36–37, 59–60, 66, 71–72, 77, 80, 89–105, 110, 115, 123, 128
Stambolić, Ivan, 54
state of nature
   in Girard's theorizing, 97–99, 124–25
   in Hobbes's theorizing, 7, 18, 29–30, 73, 97–99, 127–28
surrendering war criminals to Hague, 77–78, 95–96, 102, 114–15, 118
Svetlana, Broz, 23
svetosavlje, as example of mechanical solidarity, 124–25
Synder, Mark, 89

Todorova, Maria, 91–93
trans-ethnic institutions, need for in Bosnia-Herzegovina, 132
transgression of burial ceremony as war crime, 20–24

United Nation officials
   misunderstanding of war, 13, 58–59, 84, 111–17
   as participants in scapegoat ritual, 103–4
   as objects of degradation ceremony, 33–34
   as witnesses to genocide, 32–34, 37, 56–58
urbicide, 44, 120
utilitarian rationality, in relation to evil, 13, 59, 87, 99, 123

Vygotsky, Lev, on innate individuality of self, 88

war criminals' abuse of language, 52–61
Weber, Max
   on charismatic authority, 85–86
   on ethical irrationality of world, 75–76
   on ideal type in social inquiry, 136
West, Rebecca, on cultural significance of mosques, 131
Western diplomats, in relation to Karadžić as charismatic figure, 86
witnessing evil, 3, 23, 27–28, 30–34, 37–38, 56–58, 74, 120, 129–30, 135

Yugoslavia, Bosnia and "Brotherhood and Unity," 7, 10, 13, 28, 71–72, 73, 116, 128, 132, 140

Žižek, Slavoj, 112
Zulfikarpašić, Adil, observations of Karadžić, 109–10
Žunec, Ozren, on war and society, 122, 127